DIFFERENT DRUMMER
Homosexuality in America

BOOKS BY ELAINE LANDAU
Child Abuse: An American Epidemic
Growing Old in America
Why Are They Starving Themselves?
  Understanding Anorexia Nervosa and Bulimia

DIFFERENT DRUMMER
Homosexuality in America

Elaine Landau

JULIAN MESSNER
New York

Published by Julian Messner,
A Division of Simon & Schuster, Inc.
Simon & Schuster Building
Rockefeller Center
1230 Avenue of the Americas
New York, New York 10020

JULIAN MESSNER and colophon are
trademarks of Simon & Schuster, Inc.

10 9 8 7 6 5 4 3 2

Manufactured in the United States of America

Library of Congress Cataloging-in-Publication Data

Landau, Elaine.
    Different drummer.

    Bibliography: p.
    Includes index.
    Summary: Discusses the emotional, social, and
physical aspects of homosexuality and the problems
encountered by homosexuals and lesbians in an antihomosexual society.
    1. Homosexuality—United States—Juvenile literature.
[1. Homosexuality] I. Title.
HQ76.26.L36 1986   306.7′66′0973   85-21679
ISBN 0-671-54997-9

For Annette Frisch

A Note from the Author

Interspersed within this text under the sections *Young Gay and Lesbian Voices* are actual interviews conducted with gay and lesbian youths. These sessions were originally taped and then later transcribed into manuscript form. Only first names have been provided in order to safeguard the privacy of these individuals, who were willing to share their experiences.

In no manner are these young people composites of any sort. Each is a separate and distinct individual with a story to tell.

CONTENTS

CHAPTER ONE

Homosexuality

Boy meets girl
They fall in love
Marry, raise a family, and live happily ever after . . .

This theme succinctly embodies the essence of romantic love in American culture. The message is so deeply woven into the fabric of our daily existence that we often may not even realize how enmeshed it is in our thinking, as well as in our expectations of ourselves and others.

• There was a papa bear, mama bear, and baby bear in the story—the perfect family.

• Five- to eight-year-old boys and girls coyly flirt and dance with one another on television commercials for children's designer sportswear.

• Magazines aimed at teen female audiences abound with advertisements for engagement rings, fine china, bridal gowns, and various bridal accessories.

*   *   *

1

The concept of the traditional American family is an integral part of the American dream; a dream that is reinforced through school texts and media images. It's a dream that smiles down on us from highway billboards. Boys and girls together—that's the way it's supposed to be. But that's not the way it is for everyone.

Homosexuals—gay and lesbian individuals—are people who feel love and attraction more strongly for members of their own sex than for those of the opposite sex. Many gays and lesbians have asserted that this is the only difference between them and their heterosexual counterparts. They stress that homosexual love relationships do not differ significantly from comparable heterosexual unions. Gays and lesbians point to the fact that homosexuals derive the same excitement and fulfillment from their romantic commitments; they also experience the difficulties common to all people involved in establishing intense emotional bonds.

Gays and lesbians are a highly diversified group. Homosexuals are both male and female, young and old, and of all nationalities and races. Many gays and lesbians feel that being homosexual is not a problem in and of itself. It is being gay or lesbian in a society laden with prejudice against even the slightest hint of homosexuality that can present difficulties.

Some individuals who are gay or lesbian realize these feelings in themselves early on and are more easily able to accept their own sexual preference and the ensuing sexual identity that unfolds for them. However, many gays and lesbians claim that acknowledging a sexual preference that differs from the norm forces them to deal with all the stereotypes, misconceptions, and prejudices that accompany this choice in our society. Besides being homosexual, gay and lesbian individuals are also integral members of our society. Raised within the same culture, gays and lesbians also learned the ugly jokes and prejudices that are commonly hurled at any ridiculed minority. Some homosexual organizations have pointed out that if a young boy at the age of six is led to believe that gays are sick degenerates, his reaction at realizing his own homosexual feelings at sixteen may generate revulsion within himself. Even if he himself hasn't held these prejudices in years, barbs of this nature can be difficult to shake from one's consciousness.

Homosexuals have acknowledged often that unlearning misinformation and misconceptions still commonly held in a society that is primarily antigay can be a long and arduous process. The young man described earlier would also have to face the reality that many people, including some he may have liked and respected over the years, will have negative attitudes toward homosexuality.

He may worry that if his real feelings are discovered, he may be rejected by people he cares about. Overnight he can become an object of scorn, lose his job, be banned from a fraternity, or be made to endure countless other indignities if someone learns that he loves a member of his own sex. The affirmation of his positive feelings may result in severe consequences. That is why some gays and lesbians feel that it is sometimes difficult to initially accept being homosexual. What they may feel inside as a happy beginning in one sense can result in some very painful endings. Many gays and lesbians have undergone an intensely personal inner struggle before coming to grips with openly being who they are.

Some homosexual organizations have pointed out that the sex education taught in schools is often not very helpful to young gays and lesbians. Usually such courses deal largely with the clinical aspects of heterosexual sex and the reproductive process. In many instances, scant attention is given to the emotional responses and give-and-take that people share with one another in sexual situations.

These groups feel that gay and lesbian young people must carve out their own identity and sexual preference within a heterosexual romantic arena in which they are outsiders. Positive role models for such young people—based on competent, successful homosexuals who lead fulfilling lives—certainly do not abound in literature or in the media. In fact, some homosexual organizations have asserted that the negative stereotypes of homosexuals perpetuated by the media—such as that of men with exaggerated feminine gestures or manly, "butch" women—may be especially disastrous to young people who feel that although they are attracted to members of their own sex, they don't wish to look like caricatures.

The vast majority of gays and lesbians claim that they did not arbitrarily decide to become homosexuals, but rather that they became more aware of and in touch with these feelings as they matured both emotionally and sexually. Many think that a young individual experiencing sexual fantasies about members of his or her own sex, or who feels romantically drawn to someone who is never supposed to be more than a friend, may feel alienated and cut off from his or her peer group. It is always difficult to be different, especially if that difference can lead to rejection.

Homosexual organizations have decried the fact that there are few guidelines for young gays and lesbians to follow as they emerge into adulthood. While heterosexual young people generally have the approval of family, friends, and society, and are encouraged to date and discover themselves, young homosexuals may be afraid to do so. Gay and lesbian individuals living in large urban areas may have an easier time meeting and socializing than those living in isolated villages and small towns. In any case, for many gay and lesbian individuals, doing what really feels right for them often takes a great deal of courage and fortitude.

Acknowledging oneself as a homosexual is not always a clear-cut issue. Overt sexuality, sexual feelings, and fantasies may span a broad range for many individuals. There are no hard and fast rules to define homosexuality. For example, is someone a homosexual if that person:

- has a dream or fantasy about a member of his or her own sex?
- has had both homosexual and heterosexual experiences?
- feels tremendously drawn to members of his or her own sex?
- experiences feelings of jealousy and hurt when a close friend of the same sex becomes romantically involved with a member of the opposite sex or feels rejected when that friend forms a friendship with another member of the same sex?
- has had only one homosexual experience?
- only dates members of the opposite sex, yet finds members of his or her own sex more exciting both physically and emotionally?

* * *

The facts and feelings involved may not always be clear. For some gays and lesbians the initial decision to act on their homosexual feelings is an intensely personal one. At times, sorting out and piecing together the new awareness that they may be experiencing can be difficult. However, many homosexual individuals claim that once a person has found the answer, he or she has found more than a path to romantic involvement. Such individuals have discovered and come to terms with an important part of themselves.

CHAPTER TWO

A Fact Sheet

1. Homosexuality has existed in every society since the time of recorded history.

One study reports that in over 60 percent of the cultures studied, homosexuality was not considered a deviation from the norm, but was regarded as an acceptable expression of sexuality.

2. In the United States alone, approximately 10 percent of the population is homosexual.

3. At this time it is still not known what factors determine whether someone will be homosexual or heterosexual.

A good deal of research has been done on the topic, but the findings are still inconclusive. Among the possibilities studied have been genetic predisposition, the prenatal environment, hormonal factors, and early childhood experiences. Although it is possible for someone with a homosexual orientation to suppress his or her feelings in an attempt to act as a heterosexual, such endeavors have generally proved unsuccessful over a prolonged period of time. The fact that an individual with a homosexual preference may be capable of forming heterosexual relationships does not mean that such relationships will be rewarding for that person or fulfill his or her needs.

4. It is not illegal to be a homosexual in the United States.

However, in some areas, there are laws against specific sexual acts commonly associated with homosexuality. Still, these same acts may also be engaged in by heterosexuals. Therefore, if these acts are to be deemed illegal, technically they should be considered so for anyone engaging in them, regardless of that person's sexual preference.

In the vast majority of cases where such laws have been enforced, they have been used almost exclusively against gay men. In such instances, these laws may have at times been used to discriminate and harass. Numerous legal institutions—among them the National Commission on Reform of the Federal Criminal Laws and the American Civil Liberties Union—have urged the repeal of such laws.

5. Homosexuality is not a mental illness, but rather a viable life-style alternative.

At one time, homosexuals were thought to be individuals exhibiting pathological behavior. As such, they were often encouraged to seek psychiatric help. Within a therapeutic setting, such individuals were helped to correct what was regarded as their problem behavior—loving another person of their own sex.

However, research completed within the last few decades has proven conclusively that homosexuals do not necessarily suffer from psychological problems. In fact, actual studies have demonstrated that there is no greater incidence of mental illness among homosexual people than among heterosexuals. An official acknowledgement of this change first came from the medical community in 1973, when the American Psychiatric

A Fact Sheet

Association removed homosexuality from the list of mental disorders in its diagnostic manual. In 1975 the American Psychological Association reaffirmed the action taken by the American Psychiatric Association and passed a resolution that stated: "Homosexuality, per se, implies no impairment in judgment, stability, reliability, or general social or vocational capabilities."

6. Homosexuals are not any more likely to molest young children than are heterosexuals.

Despite the myth that gays and lesbians habitually seduce small children into clandestine sexual encounters, there is no evidence to validate such an assumption. On the contrary, according to the Department of Health, Education, and Welfare's National Center on Child Abuse and Neglect, over 90 percent of all sexual abuse to children is committed by heterosexual men against young girls.

7. Homosexuals are not limited to careers in fashion, theater, or the arts.

Accomplished and talented gay and lesbian professionals may be found in almost every area of achievement. This partial listing of only a few of the many gay/lesbian professional organizations serves to highlight the substantial diversity.

Gay People in Medicine Task Force
National Association of Lesbian & Gay Filmmakers
National Lawyers' Guild Gay Caucus
Gay Teachers
Federal Lesbian & Gay Employees
Gay Academic Union
Gay Officers' Action League, Inc.
Gay Caucus for the Modern Languages
National Center for Gay Ministry

Gay Nurses Alliance
National Caucus of Gay and Lesbian Counselors
Triangle Area Gay Scientists
Workforce (lesbian tradeswomen and craftswomen)

There are many more gay and lesbian professional organizations in addition to those listed above.
There are also gay/lesbian student groups, gay/les-
bian teacher groups, and gay/lesbian business and
professional organizations too numerous to mention in
almost every major American city.

Gay and lesbian workers and professionals may be
found alongside their heterosexual counterparts prac-
tically everywhere in the world of work. Among the
numbers of especially prominent gay and lesbian individuals of the past and present:

Sappho—Greek poetess (approximately 600 B.C.)
Virginia Woolf—author (1882–1941)
Bessie Smith—singer (1894–1937)
Janis Joplin—singer (1943–1970)
Aristotle—Greek philosopher (384–322 B.C.)
Alexander the Great—ruler (356–323 B.C.)
Walt Whitman—poet (1819–1892)
Tennessee Williams—playwright (1911–1983)
David Bowie—singer (1947–)
Elton John—singer (1947–)

CHAPTER THREE

Young Gay and Lesbian Voices:
"I Loved Lonnie"

"I think I had an awareness that I was a lesbian from an early age. At first, when I was a very young child, I might not have known the word 'lesbian.' Yet I do remember that later when I learned what being a lesbian was and what it made you in our society, I knew I couldn't accept who I was just then.

"Still, I was always drawn to other girls. To me, they seemed so soft and lovely—like the beautiful dolls my parents gave me for Christmas. I remember how some [girls] looked so pretty in their colorful party dresses with ribbons streaming down the back of their hair. The fact that my mother had always insisted on dressing me for festive occasions in the same manner somehow never seemed to register in my mind. It was almost as if I didn't see or care what I was wearing. I just wanted to admire them.

"These feelings grew and led to what became a very tortured girlhood for me. I was in love with every best friend I had through the years. Of course, I never called it love, never even dared to think of it as such. Still, I always felt that I wanted and needed to be very special to my treasured girlfriends.

"If they placed another friend before me, I was crushed. If they invited another girl to go shopping with us, I hated it. I never uttered a word of protest, but it was as if my heart had been cut with a knife. There was never anything overtly sexual going on between those special girlfriends and myself, but at different times in my life I cherished each of them and viewed others in our small social circle as intruders.

"As time passed, my friends became interested in boys, but I didn't. Afraid of what that might really make me, I pretended to be. This didn't prove to be tremendously helpful though, because it seemed that most of the boys weren't going to stand in line to get a date with me anyway.

"None of the really popular boys I might have wanted to go out with ever paid any attention to me. There was one boy, Kenny, who did claim to be in love with me. His romantic interest in me lasted for over two years, and the whole situation was pathetic. Kenny was about four inches shorter than I was and about twenty-five pounds overweight. I may have spent some time with him, but I never felt anything close to love or even attraction for Kenny. Kenny became a good friend, while my girlfriends remained my love objects, adored from afar.

"Things took a turn for the worse when junior high ended and we went on to high school. It was a large high school, with kids attending from several surrounding suburban areas. It seemed as if there were millions of new kids swarming the halls, classrooms, and cafeteria. In any case, it was there that I saw Lonnie for the first time.

"Lonnie was a dream girl. I think she must have epitomized everyone's ideal of young womanhood. Lonnie was tall and gorgeous with a terrific figure, a smooth complexion, and a smile that sparkled. She had magnificent, long, blonde hair. I never found out if she really was the natural blonde she claimed to be, but it didn't matter. She looked wonderful.

"Now Lonnie was no ordinary teen glamour queen. She was as beautiful inside as she was on the outside. Picture an innocent Playboy bunny with a feminist viewpoint—that was Lonnie. Or a fairy princess who was as good as she was beautiful. That was Lonnie too.

"Lonnie was popular. Some of the girls she hung around with admired her, while others were just green with envy. Just about every boy at school was crazy about her. I found myself in a very difficult predicament, because I was hopelessly in love with Lonnie as well.

"How can I describe what it felt like to be fifteen years old and in love with another girl—a girl who thought of me only as a sweet, solicitous friend and had no idea of the uneasy awakenings and tumultuous feelings she was causing me.

"I thought of Lonnie as a wondrous human being in many different ways. Sometimes I looked at her long, straight, sparkling strands of blonde hair and thought of her as a stream of sunshine. Pink was Lonnie's favorite color and she wore a different shade of it just about every day.

"Lonnie and I became good friends because it was easy to be friends with her. Warm and outgoing, Lonnie defied the stereotype of the snobby, aloof beauty. Lots of people wanted to be friends with Lonnie, but perhaps because I tried hardest, I was selected to be among her choice friends.

"It was I who always bought her the best birthday gift, offered her my finished homework to copy, flattered her, and ran little errands for her. Maybe I did too much. At times my perhaps over-solicitous behavior towards her embarrassed both Lonnie and myself. She really had never demanded anything of me. Lonnie was just happy to be my friend.

"Still, I wanted to do everything for Lonnie. It was the only way I could express what I felt for her in a socially acceptable manner. I knew that I was crazy about her, but I really wasn't sure what it all meant.

"Was I a lesbian? I couldn't cope with even thinking about that possibility. If it were true, and people found out, I was sure that I'd be an outcast. People would make fun of me. I was certain that no one would want to be my friend. Lonnie liked guys a lot; I thought that she'd probably be scared of me. So if I ever even tried to tell her what I was beginning to be sure she really meant to me, I was certain that Lonnie would be lost to me forever.

"I didn't know any lesbians, and at that point in my life I wasn't completely positive that I was one. How could I be certain? I know that I didn't look the way I thought a lesbian would look. I wasn't the beauty queen type that Lonnie was, but there was certainly nothing 'butch' or mannish about my appearance. Besides, everyone thought Lonnie, who had enraptured me so, was as adorable as a china doll. Would a lesbian be in love with this type of girl? I just didn't know.

"Still, as time passed, I simply couldn't deny what I was feeling and what those feelings probably meant. The privileges that Lonnie so freely granted me, that of brushing out her long, blonde hair or of sitting next to her in the cafeteria, were worth more to me than a month's allowance.

"Of course, through all this I had to try to keep up some sort of facade. My parents wanted me to be interested in boys, so I continued to date Kenny. We double-dated a lot with Lonnie and whoever her current boyfriend was at the time.

"This really proved to be quite humorous, because I was certain that Kenny had secretly fallen in love with Lonnie too. I was going out with Kenny so that I could be with Lonnie most Saturday nights, and I wondered if he were going out with me for the same reason.

"Things went on very much in this manner throughout our high school years. Lonnie was always invited to everything, and whenever possible she arranged to have me come along. For years I felt like her trusted bridesmaid, when inside I longed to be the groom. I felt that I constantly had to be on guard, always careful not to be discovered.

"If I grabbed Lonnie's hand while running across the street, I had to be certain never to hold it too tightly or too long, even though I felt I so needed the touch of her. I wanted to do everything for her and be everything to her, but sometimes I forced myself to hold back. It was essential that neither Lonnie, nor anyone else for that matter, ever suspect that something was wrong.

"I thought I'd die when we graduated, and Lonnie and I went our separate ways: she to marry a local real estate broker and I to college in New York City. I thought that a part of me would never be the same. I felt as if the sun would never shine as brightly in New York City as it had on Lonnie's shiny, blonde California hair.

"However, in reality, leaving Lonnie and coming to New York City actually afforded me a tremendous sense of relief. I came to grips with who I really was and decided that for me the hiding would be over forever. I joined a gay/lesbian student organization on campus and made many new and wonderful friends. I learned that lesbians look as diverse as heterosexual women. Some are very attractive, others are not. "Today I am very much in love with a young woman I met at college. For the most part I've forgotten all about Lonnie, but I'll never forget the tormented adolescent years I spent in silence, hiding my feelings, hiding my pain, because it simply wasn't acceptable for me to be who I was. There weren't any role models or accessible social outlets for young homosexuals where I came from. I hope all that changes in the future. It hurts too much to stay in hiding."

CHAPTER FOUR

The Roots of Homophobia

Faggot, pansy, dyke, queer, lesi . . .
The above derogatory labels, and their acceptance in our culture, serve as a verbal expression of an overall societal prejudice against homosexuals. While it is true that gays and lesbians comprise a distinct minority within our society, and that historically minority groups have been used as scapegoats, the revulsion towards homosexuals and homosexual behavior appears to be particularly widespread and virulent.

This reaction against homosexuality, which has so often resulted in both blatant and subtle forms of discrimination, has come to be known as homophobia. Today, many psychotherapists believe that part of what causes someone to become homophobic may be an unconscious reaction to that person's own fear of being homosexual.

Those who take an unusually fierce stand against the expression of homosexuality in others are at times actually fighting against such impulses in themselves. Strong verbal denouncements of homosexuality help to reinforce such persons' own denial to themselves that they might in any way experience a feeling that could be considered homosexual.

The fires of homophobia may also be fanned by religious beliefs. There are direct and explicit condemnations of homosexuality in the Bible. Prejudice and oppression against homosexuals have always been at their height when reinforced by the stance of religious leaders of the period. According to the Christian doctrine, sex was to exist for the purpose of procreation. Sexual pleasure in and of itself was condemned, and in an effort to reinforce its edict, the church developed strict codes of behavior. Many sexual acts were banned, as it was believed that the participants might derive enjoyment from them. The fact that offspring could not be produced through homosexual relationships further emphasized that such liaisons existed solely for pleasure, and therefore were especially abhorrent to God and the church.

To make certain that its prohibitions were adhered to, the church set up its own courts to deal with offenders. Throughout history, thousands of individuals who engaged in homosexual acts were executed. In the minds of the public, the concept of the homosexual as a sinner was therefore further underscored by the authority of the church. Some individuals still hold this view today. Others who do not believe that sex is solely for the purpose of reproduction persist in regarding the homosexual as someone who has sinned against both God and the community.

Another factor inherent in the widespread existence of homophobia is the perception of the homosexual's life style as an arrogant challenge to the structure of our society. Individuals who do not wholly embrace the mainstream values of any society are often viewed as trying to undermine it. Differing views, other standards of morality, as well as alternative life styles, are often looked at suspiciously by those who follow the dictates of the majority.

It is often theorized that the homosexual male may serve as a threat to the masculine identity of some heterosexual males who may have put a great deal of time, effort, and money into developing a strong "macho" image. As a part of this "macho mystique" usually entails developing a certain prowess with women, the homosexual's lack of interest in such matters may seem to some as challenging the inherent worthiness of such pursuits. To some people, homosexual males may seem disdainful of achieving manhood in a heterosexual world. If the fact that such men exist makes some heterosexual males question the values and rewards they so vigorously pursue, the homosexual's way of life may be unconsciously perceived as a threat to the heterosexual's life style.

Homosexual men and women who are not striving for traditional heterosexual marriage may present a difficult challenge for some elements of our society that, for economic reasons, wish to unify and underscore the goals of the majority. For example, most products are marketed to appeal to heterosexual families. Often, breakfast cereal or juice commercials feature a mother, father, and two children seated around a breakfast table happily enjoying their morning meal.

The subtle background message is that of a typical American family enjoying good food while growing together. As of yet, there are no breakfast commercials featuring two lesbians fixing waffles for breakfast or showing a young gay couple purchasing their first home in the suburbs. Manufacturers of children's toys,

19

clothing, furnishings, school supplies, and baby diapers are just a sample of the industries perpetuated by sexual reproduction.

Laws, societal standards, and social institutions are centered around heterosexual couples as well. Homosexual couples cannot legally marry. The federal tax structure, which is designed to reflect either married or single status, does not recognize the "nonlegal" marriages of homosexuals who live together for a lifetime as though they were married. Our society is so pervasively heterosexual in its outlook that at best the homosexual is regarded as someone who will never quite fit into the mainstream, and at worst as an object of ridicule and scorn.

The nuclear family unit is a cherished institution in America. To many individuals, having children helps to insure their immortality. Their fear of death is eased by the belief that they will live on through their children. Homosexual relationships, which do not engender offspring, may serve as a distressing reminder to some people of the finite nature of life and their own mortality.

In addition, many people feel that they sacrifice a great deal for their children. Infants nourished on a four-hour feeding schedule disrupt the sleep of their new parents; parents worry about their children when they are away from home; money that might have been used for the parents' entertainment is channelled to meet college tuition expenses. Many parents justify such inconveniences because they believe that the family unit is more important than individual gratification. Childless couples defy this pattern of existence, and thus to some may seem to be challenging the value of such sacrifice. The leisure time and lesser expenses of such couples may serve as a source of envy to some people as well.

Our society operates on the false assumption that everyone is basically striving for his or her share of the same advantages. However, a heterosexual marriage leading to reproduction is not a dream shared by homosexuals. Therefore, homosexuals are condemned because they are different. The resulting discrimination against them is justified by commonly shared misconceptions.

Without any evidence to support such misconceptions, homosexuals are thought to be untrustworthy, excessively interested in sexual liaisons, unable to form lasting relationships, flighty, and superficial. It is commonly thought by many heterosexuals that homosexual men hate women, and that lesbians despise men. Lesbians are supposedly rageful and extremely aggressive. However, no scientific data exists to document any of these statements.

Homosexuals defy conventionality, and as a result they are victimized.

CHAPTER FIVE

Life Styles and Families

There isn't just one homosexual life style. The same diversity reflected among heterosexuals is found among gays and lesbians. Some homosexual individuals, not unlike their heterosexual counterparts, choose to live alone without forming a long-term, romantic commitment. These people may continue dating a number of people over a period of years. Others choose to couple. Some gay and lesbian couples may remain together for only a few months, while others have been together for over fifty years. In many ways a homosexual couple is very much like a heterosexual couple. However, in some respects, the gay or lesbian couple will encounter different experiences.

One of the special problems that may confront gay or lesbian couples stems from the degree to which the two partners may have "come out," or publicly acknowledged their homosexuality. Some gays and lesbians have said that open acknowledgment may bring the benefits of a wonderful sense of freedom and a boost in self-respect, as well as the knowledge that one is helping to make it acceptable for other gays and lesbians to live freely. These positives must be carefully balanced against the possible negative consequences that may have to be faced in openly revealing oneself as a member of a discriminated-against sexual minority. The factors influencing each individual's choice may differ due to personal circumstances.

When a gay or lesbian individual is part of a couple, the degree to which he or she may decide to come out will have ramifications on that person's partner. Those who are comfortable being themselves in both their private and professional lives may feel quite put off by a lover who may be at a very different stage of coming out, and has requested that the true nature of their relationship be kept hidden.

A gay or lesbian individual who has completely come out may not have a great deal of patience and respect for others who are unable to respect his or her life choices. It is not uncommon for difficulties to arise between couples regarding how their respective families are to be handled. Often a gay or lesbian individual may feel torn between loyalty to biological family members who are unaware of his or her sexual preference and loyalty to his or her lover. Similar conflicts may also arise if one member of a gay or lesbian couple wishes to attend gay or lesbian social functions with his or her lover, or wants to become active in a gay/lesbian rights group and the lover is not prepared to reveal the true nature of their relationship. When such differences exist, they tend to add to the stresses that are brought to bear on a gay or lesbian couple, as illustrated in the following story.

Jane, a lesbian who had chosen to conceal her sexual identity from her colleagues, was selected by her co-workers to give a bridal shower for another staff member who was getting married. Doris, the lover with whom she lived, worked in another department of the same company and knew many of Jane's colleagues. Doris was open about being a lesbian, but because Jane worked for the same company and didn't want to reveal her sexual identity, the two women had made certain that no one thought they were any more to each other than casual friends. Although Doris would have preferred not to be involved in a secret relationship, she respected Jane's right to privacy.

However, having to host the bridal shower in their home did put a strain on the women. Doris felt pressured to hide most of her belongings, placing some of the most obvious objects in a neighbor's apartment for the evening. Although she did attend the party, she had to pretend that she was there simply as one of the guests. Both women felt embarrassed by the whole situation, but the evening really worsened when Doris's brother called long distance from Hawaii and Jane had to tell him that he had reached a wrong number.

Even minor incidents like this can gnaw at the trust and loyalty generated between members of gay and lesbian couples. Many homosexual couples have stressed that such situations need to be balanced by a strong foundation of love and commitment between the individuals involved.

Some lesbian feminists have pointed out that lesbian couples are often forced to deal with special stresses not shared by their male homosexual counterparts. In addition to having to contend with the prevalent negative attitudes toward homosexuality, lesbians must also cope with discrimination against women. The pressures that help to relegate women to a position of second-class citizenship range from economic discrimination in the workplace to being portrayed as sex objects in the media. In addition, women also become the victims of such blatant acts of hostility as rape, sadistic pornography, and wife abuse. According to noted pediatrician Benjamin Spock, "A little girl is treated and molded differently from a little boy from the day she is born." Most traditional fairy tales offer examples of pretty heroines who are rewarded for their good looks and sweet dispositions by marriage to a prince. Sleeping Beauty sleeps her life away for a hundred years. During this period she remains inactive, passive, and totally unable to help herself—she can only be reawakened by a prince's kiss. Cinderella is hardly a successful saga of a woman leading a full and independent life without the assistance of a male. She can only be rescued from a life of drudgery by a prince who falls in love with her at a ball. Lazy Mary and frightened Little Miss Muffet are not portrayed as brave, resourceful women.

As little girls, many women were given dolls instead of doctor kits to play with. At about twelve or thirteen, tomboys begin to lose their charm, and their behavior is considered inappropriate.

If the basic premise of a society is that each woman should eventually be asked by a man to be his wife and the mother of his children, she must make herself desirable in order to be selected. Girls learn to giggle at boys' jokes, look pretty, and not challenge the boys in their science and math classes. They learn that a girl who knows how to help, please, and flatter a man is considered desirable and charming, even if she has to forsake a bit of her identity and dignity to do so.

A lesbian grows up in a society that demands that a woman eventually team up with a man at some point in her life if she is to be considered a successful person in step with her culture. Pressure of this nature may be burdensome to any young woman, but especially so for a lesbian, who may have never wanted to share her life with a man to begin with.

In loving another woman, the lesbian may be forced to contend with the assertion by others that she is involved in an "unnatural" relationship as well as the painful insinuation that she only chose another woman because she was unable to "get a man."

A woman who chooses another woman for her mate may also find that her lover is considered less than ideal because she lacks many of the positive attributes generally ascribed to men. For example, many people believe a woman needs a man to protect her. Often a woman accompanied by a man will not be as vulnerable to the vulgar remarks, propositions, or even attacks by other males as she might be if she were alone or accompanied by another woman. This is because a woman with a man is usually perceived as belonging to him, a concept that may be respected by other males.

However, the sense of security that some women may experience being attached to a male may not be based on reality. Statistically, as many married women become rape victims as do single women. In addition, a woman who depends upon a man to protect her from being accosted, and therefore never feels it necessary to learn any form of self-defense, may find herself in a more vulnerable position when she happens to be out alone.

On the other hand, a woman who feels entirely responsible for her own protection might be more likely to make herself as knowledgeable as possible. The notion that a woman with a man will always be protected is further belied by the thousands of women who annually are victims of wife abuse. A woman married to an abusive man rarely finds someone who will protect her from his assaultive behavior.

Special difficulties can arise for both lesbian and gay couples when children are involved. Many lesbians and gay men have had children either before realizing that they were homosexual or before coming out. Such individuals may be homosexuals, but they are parents as well.

Other gays and lesbians who were not involved in intimate relationships with members of the opposite sex may still long to be involved in child-rearing. Some gay men have adopted children, as have some lesbians. Other lesbians have given birth through artificial insemination.

It is difficult for some people to imagine lesbians as mothers. However, a gay or lesbian parent is very much like a heterosexual parent. Both are subject to the same pressures of work and money, anxieties about their children, and the typical household conflicts and squabbling that occur in most families. Studies by researchers Kirkpatrick, Smith, and Ray, published in the *American Journal of Orthopsychiatry*, which compared a group of heterosexual mothers to a comparable group of lesbian mothers, have indicated that the similarities found in the two types of parenting situations far exceed the differences.

In both groups, the major problems proved to be finding adequate child care for their offspring and coping with financial pressures. Although a number of the lesbian mothers indicated that they experienced some guilt over the possibility that their sexual preference might in some way have an adverse effect on their children, the researchers found, in studying the children, that their parent's homosexuality did not have a negative impact on their overall development.

The bulk of the research demonstrated that the difficulties experienced by lesbian and gay parents did not usually come from the parents themselves, but rather from negative societal attitudes and discrimination against the homosexual parent. In a survey of children of gay and lesbian parents conducted by researcher K. Lewis and published in the journal *Social Work,* the overwhelming majority indicated that the breakup of their parents' marriage was significantly more upsetting to them than learning that their parent was homosexual. Among the children studied, there was tremendous variation in their reactions upon learning that their parent was gay or lesbian. These reactions ranged from such negative sentiments as, "If you're one of those, I'm just going to die," to a sense of acceptance. Several children felt that now that the truth was out in the open, their parent might feel freer to be himself or herself, and that this would make life easier for everyone in the household.

While some children expressed their wish for parents who were more like "everyone else," others stated that they couldn't tell the difference between mothers who were lesbians and those who lived with men. These children simply perceived the lesbian women as mothers. As one seven-year-old girl put it, "Lesbians are ladies who love you, and take care of you, and make sure that nothing bad ever happens to you."

It was found that younger children were generally initially more accepting of their parent's homosexuality than adolescents. Teenagers, who appeared to be more preoccupied with conformity and adhering to

29

peer group norms, often found it more difficult to accept a parent who was different.

How the issue of parental homosexuality is handled in the school may greatly depend on the individual value systems of the teachers. Unfortunately, in some situations, teachers have openly condemned homosexuality, and have thus intensified the difficulties faced by the children from homosexual home environments.

Other teachers have chosen to completely avoid the issue; still others have advocated tolerance. One third-grade teacher effectively rescued a student from the taunts of her classmates. On the day that the class created Mother's Day cards, the girl had announced that she needed materials to make two cards since she had two lesbian mommies and she loved them both. When the other students teased her, the teacher ended their remarks by saying, "We must all learn to be tolerant of others. There is more than one way to live and to give love. No one can be considered to be a loving person if that individual is incapable of respecting the differences of others."

Gay and lesbian parents may vary in the extent to which they are open with their children about their sexuality. Some believe that it is essential for their children to know who their parent really is. These individuals may feel it unhealthy for both the child and parent to live in an atmosphere of pretense. However, due to the prejudices within our society, some lesbian and gay parents have found it necessary to use discretion in certain situations pertaining to their children. As one lesbian mother stated:

"In loving another woman, I've made a life choice that's right for me. Although I've had to face discrimination in acknowledging my homosexuality in a number of areas of my life, the joy and fulfillment I derive from my mate more than counterbalances this.

"However, I have two children from a prior marriage. Although I thought I loved my husband at the time of our marriage, and tried to go on sharing my life with him, something inside that was somehow always denied kept gnawing at me. At last I decided that I had to own up to the reality that I was a lesbian, and that I had to live my life that way if I was ever to know any sense of inner peace.

"When I left my husband, I took our two children with me. I have a boy who is now six and a little girl who is four. They are sweet, beautiful, children and I care for them very much, as does my new lover and roommate, Linda. The children share their lives with Linda; she is a loving and integral part of their everyday existence. She taught my son how to pitch a baseball, and my daughter claims that Linda tells the best bedtime stories she ever heard.

"Right now, the children sort of think of Linda as an aunt. To them, she's just someone nice who lives in their home and shares good as well as bad times with them. The children know that Linda is special to me, as she is to them, but at this time they are still unaware of the sexual bond that exists between us.

"Linda and I have decided to let the children know the true nature of our relationship as soon as they are old enough to understand. We are not ashamed of being lesbians, but feel we would be ashamed of living a lie in front of our own family.

"This decision was not really difficult to arrive at. We have to be what we are and we want our children to see that their parents or caretakers have the courage to stand up for what they believe in. We only hope that from our example, the children may one day derive the strength to stand by whatever choices they make that may be right for them, even if those dreams are not quite in keeping with the views of the majority.

"We know we want to do this, but we do worry about the ramifications our decision may have on the children. Living and loving as lesbians was a choice that Linda and I made. It was not the choice of the children —they may grow up to be either heterosexual or homosexual. We sometimes wrestle with the possibility that, after learning that we are lesbians and perhaps inadvertently revealing this fact to their friends, our children will be humiliated for something over which they have no control.

"Although we are concerned about this possibility, in discussing the problem with other gay and lesbian parents, we learned that it is something that can be overcome. In telling their children about their homosexuality, gay and lesbian parents often explain that they want to be honest with their children about who they are, but they also feel it necessary to warn their children about the discrimination against gays and lesbians in our society. Some of the parents may suggest that their offspring only share this information with others using discretion."

A number of homosexual parents have suggested that their children's experiences may also be influenced by where they live and the nature of their social circle. In large urban areas where homosexual parents may have the opportunity to join gay and lesbian organizations, their children may have more of a chance to become acquainted with other families like their own. Gay and lesbian parents who live in suburban or rural areas may find this more difficult to do.

Not every homosexual parent lives as part of a couple. Some of the problems faced by gay and lesbian parents are the same as those experienced by hetero-sexual single parents. Dating, and perhaps sometimes bringing home a special lover to meet the children, can cause the same feelings of jealousy, resentment, and displacement as experienced by offspring in a hetero-sexual single-parent family when Dad introduces his new girlfriend or when Mom announces that her boyfriend is moving in.

Until they actually accept the reality of a divorce, young children who lived in a two-parent family may yearn to have their parents reunited. Many children fantasize about being back in their former family situation. The new person introduced into the family circle by their parent becomes a painful reminder that this is not going to happen. On the other hand, children who grew up having only one parent may have a tendency to become overly possessive of that parent, and view a new person entering the family situation as an intruder.

The young person may eventually come to accept the new person as someone having the potential to bring even more love and resources to the family. However, often a rough early stage is to be expected before everyone comes together. The children of a homosexual parent experience the same disruption in their lives when such changes occur, as do the children of heterosexual single parents.

Some gay and lesbian parents have had to face considerable discrimination from members of their own biological families. After learning that a family member is homosexual, heterosexual brothers, sisters, and even parents have offered to raise the homosexual's child in their own home. These relatives often will argue that the child has the right to grow up in what they regard as a "normal" home environment. Although numerous gay and lesbian organizations have pointed out that there is no data to suggest that these children would have brighter futures if brought up by their heterosexual relatives, often gay and lesbian parents are prodded by their families to give up their children.

Some gay and lesbian parents have faced the threat of custody battles after revealing their sexual preference. This has been especially true for lesbian mothers who were formerly married to heterosexual men. Many of these women were excellent mothers both when married and divorced. However, their former spouses have brought them to court in custody suits, attempting to take away their children on the grounds that because they are lesbians they are unfit as mothers. Attorneys for these women routinely argue that there is no conclusive evidence to support the notion that lesbians are any less proficient at mothering than are heterosexual women.

The majority of gay and lesbian groups offering legal advice to homosexual parents who wish to retain custody of their children suggest that whenever possible, it is best to stay out of court. Case verdicts reveal that throughout the years the judicial system has been largely unreceptive to changing life styles. In general, society tends to frown on child-rearing environments outside of legalized, heterosexual marriages. Gay and lesbian groups have argued that judges, who are given a great deal of power in settling custody disputes, have not always been able to leave their own prejudices out of the courtroom, as has been reflected through the many prejudicial decisions involving the rights of gay and lesbian parents. Although some of these unfair decisions have been overturned by higher courts, gay and lesbian groups stress that many have not. They further point out that, to make matters worse, blatantly discriminatory decisions in some instances are still being made today.

The question in determining custody in a divorce or separation is supposedly based on the issue of what is in the child's best interest. This standard gives the judge tremendous latitude in his or her decision making. Gay and lesbian groups point to the fact that the judge may determine that just about anything can be considered relevant to the child's welfare, including the sexual preference of the parent. They feel that a judge who approaches a custody case with preconceived notions of the effects of homosexuality on children, rather than with actual facts, may tend to fall back on his or her own prejudices.

Some homosexual organizations stress that since gay and lesbian parents may often not be readily discernible in our society, many judges know very little about them. Although there are gays and lesbians in most professions, few judges—or anyone else for that matter—would be able to pick them out among their own colleagues. As a result, the gay and lesbian groups believe that court decisions may often reflect the myths and stereotypes about homosexuality prevalent in our society.

For numerous gay and lesbian parents, custody battles have proven to be an expensive and exhausting ordeal. One lesbian mother involved in an extensive and bitter custody suit lost her daughter and was left with debts of several thousand dollars. The suit lasted for over eighteen months and had required a number of court appearances for both the mother and child. Many people familiar with the case believe that the judge had decided that the woman was an unfit mother before any evidence had been presented. Her former husband's case consisted largely of stereotyped myths about lesbians with which the judge seemed to agree. Although two court-appointed psychiatrists and a social worker gave evidence that the girl was well adjusted, and that her mother had been an excellent parent, their expert opinions were totally ignored. Also disregarded was the testimony of the child herself, who unequivocally stated that she wished to remain with her mother. Throughout the trial, the mother's ability to provide her daughter with the emotional care and love needed by the child was hardly considered. The woman's lawyer said that his client had never had a chance, that she was really on trial for being a lesbian.

In some instances, the grandparents challenge the gay or lesbian parent's right in court to custody of their grandchildren. A Georgia court awarded custody of an eight-year-old girl to the child's paternal grandparents after her parents divorced because the girl's natural mother was a lesbian. The judge felt that the mother's life style would have an unwholesome effect on the child, despite the fact that a court-appointed psychiatrist had testified that the child (who had already been staying with her biological mother) was well adjusted and appeared to be properly cared for. Even the child's father had indicated in court that his former wife had been an outstanding mother, and that he would prefer to see his daughter remain with her mother rather than be placed with his own parents. However, his sentiments as well as those of the child were ignored.

Courts have substantial power in granting parental visitation rights. These rights determine when a parent is permitted to see his or her children. Often courts will award visitation rights with special conditions attached. Homosexual groups point to the fact that at times both gay and lesbian parents have been forbidden to live with their lovers if they wish to have their children visit them in their homes. If the homosexual parent has a lover, the parent may not be permitted to see the children in the lover's presence. Homosexual groups have documented numerous custody cases in which homosexual parents have not been permitted to see their children under any circumstances in the presence of another adult who is not heterosexual.

Although numerous homosexual parents claim to have borne the brunt of prejudice in custody proceedings, there have been instances in which such disputes were settled on the basis of sheer factual evidence. Some gays and lesbians are heartened by the fact that court decisions of this nature may be on the rise. In a famous lesbian custody case (involving a trial with twenty-one witnesses and eleven psychiatrists), two lesbians were permitted to retain custody of a total of eight children between them. They were also allowed to continue living in a combined residence as one family. However, in an appeal of the decision, the women were ordered to live separately, although each was still permitted to retain custody of her own children.

In the Southwest a court awarded custody of three children to the lesbian lover of a mother who had committed suicide. The two women had lived together with the children as a family for over twelve years. The children had come to regard their mother's mate as their own parent as well, since a strong emotional bond had evolved over the years between the household members. The only other available guardian for the children had been the mother's sister.

Homosexual rights groups have strenuously pointed to the fact that prejudices and stereotypes have no place in the courtrooms of a democratic society. They stress that at this time there is no evidence to indicate that the children of heterosexual parents are better adjusted or lead more fulfilling lives than children raised by a homosexual parent or caretaker. Attorneys for such groups have argued that homosexual parents are entitled by law to the same rights as heterosexual parents to love, raise, and care for their offspring.

According to the Supreme Court, the right of a parent to keep and raise his or her children has been deemed as "essential to the orderly pursuit of happiness" and "far more precious than property rights." The state may only interfere with the parent-child bond when the child's welfare is in jeopardy. Gays and lesbians say that it is not an issue of whom a parent chooses to love, but rather a question of can the parent provide a loving, nurturing, and protective home environment for the child.

CHAPTER SIX

Young Gay and Lesbian Voices: Jeff

"In high school it was hard for me to accept that I was different; I mean really different from the other guys I hung around with. I didn't want to be different, and I certainly didn't want to be gay. I remember longing to be part of the whole macho vision—to drive a fast car, drink beer, conquer women, the whole bit.

"I wanted to be like everybody else, and even then I thought that in many ways I really wasn't very different from the others. I drag raced and was known to have gotten really drunk at parties. But the girl thing—that was becoming an insurmountable problem for me, one that I didn't know how to escape.

"When we were younger, you really didn't have to do much with girls. I mean, we teased them, yelled out after them, and mostly just danced and fooled around with them at parties. It usually started when we'd get together in a group. You really didn't have to take part directly, just being there made you a part of the action. Of course, a few of the guys went steady, but not that many. In any case, you could easily get along by just hanging out.

"Girls didn't seem to matter to me. Hanging out with the guys was what really counted, just being around them meant everything to me. I was comfortable with them while the girls always seemed like outsiders. I had two best friends for whom I especially cared. Often I thought that I would have died for them if the need had arisen. After a time, I knew that I was going to have to admit to myself what I had secretly suspected for years. My feelings for these guys were different and much stronger than what they felt for me or for any other man, for that matter. I had to face it—I was probably gay.

"It wasn't really a revelation to me. I know that I had been trying to deny my feelings for a long time. The truth of it was that I was drawn to other guys. I had felt a passion for certain men that I had never experienced for a woman in my life.

"At times I felt as though I lacked the emotional resources to cope with what I was going through. I remember one time when my friend Terry, whom I had always regarded as being just about the best-looking guy in the world, grabbed me on the court after I had scored a basket, a shiver ran through my entire body. I was even afraid to shower after games with the other guys, for fear of getting an erection and having the truth about myself exposed.

"I wasn't prepared to accept myself as gay, and sometimes I felt as if I might be the only gay teenager in the entire world. No one in my immediate circle of friends and acquaintances was gay. I also knew of no homosexual relatives or teachers. The stereotype of the limp-wristed guy in woman's clothing really disgusted me, and made me loathe who I thought I was.

"It wasn't until several years later that I was able to come in contact with homosexual men from all walks of life, whom I both liked and respected. In the meantime, I was in a small high school in a small town with no one to turn to and desperately afraid of what lay ahead.

"And then, of course, there was Marie, the daughter of my father's business partner. For years our parents had jokingly suggested how wonderful it would be if we married and together carried on the joint family business. Unfortunately, Marie thought I was cute and felt all too comfortable in her role of pursuing me. When I never showed even the slightest sign of interest in Marie, my parents always made excuses for me, saying I was shy or a late bloomer.

"Still, I continually felt pressured—by my parents, who really wanted me to date, by Marie, to take an interest in her, even by the guys, who wanted to double date or perhaps just talk about girls with me.

"What was I to do? I was aware of an ever-growing sense of desperation. Everyone around me appeared to be emerging as heterosexual adults, while I felt stunted in my sexuality and relationships with others. I might have been a high school junior, but socially it was as if I were in the seventh grade.

"I decided once and for all that I was going to try to beat the rap. Even though everything inside of me told me that this would never work, I was determined to remake myself into a typical heterosexual male. I hoped that if I tried really hard to redirect my feelings, maybe then I could turn things around.

"However, my efforts failed dismally. For one thing, I soon learned that it's next to impossible to interest girls in you when you're not really interested in them.

I think they sense that you're not for real. So instead I decided to take out Marie. I thought that it would be easy, since she was already interested in me. Besides, it seemed to do wonders for my parents. My father was so thrilled he hinted that he would buy me a new car.

"Unfortunately, my date with Marie turned out to be the ultimate mishap. The experience made TV disaster movies look mild. If I had found Marie to be pushy in our initial encounters with our families, she proved to be a thousand times worse on a date. Although Marie was considered pretty by some, I had never found her so, and I was hoping to delay the physical aspects of our new relationship until we got to know one another better.

"No such luck. Marie was as aggressive sexually as she was in every other way. She was all over me at the movie, and riding home in the car she kept grabbing at my thigh. I really felt scared. I knew by then that there was no hope of my getting an erection with Marie, and I was worried about how much of all this she would relate to kids we both knew from school.

"To camouflage this embarrassing reality, I made some excuse about having to be in early that night, and drove Marie directly home. Fortunately, she hadn't actually touched my private parts and I could only hope that she hadn't realized that her amorous gestures had been wasted on me.

"I knew that night I couldn't continue with this charade. I had never felt so apprehensive and ill at ease in my life. I told my parents that I wasn't going to ask Marie out again because I had found her personality too overwhelming. My parents—heartened by the fact that I had at least demonstrated some interest in any girl—were sympathetic, and assured me that I'd soon find another young lady to date.

"I knew that it wasn't going to happen, but I quietly lived with their expectations, and sometimes hated myself for being the son who I knew would eventually have to smash their dreams."

CHAPTER SEVEN

Homosexuality and Mental Health

For most of the past two thousand years, homosexuality has borne numerous negative labels, ranging from being called a crime to its classification as a disease. When early religious authorities proclaimed sexuality that was not for the express purpose of procreation to be a violation against God, homosexuality came to be viewed as a dangerous alternative to the task of human survival. As a result, homosexuals became the victims of harsh repressive measures. Such attacks were often spearheaded by political authorities as well as by religious leaders.

This antihomosexual bias became securely rooted within cultural foundations, and was reflected in all aspects of society. Unfortunately, such prejudices served as the backdrop for the scientific study of homosexuality that began in the nineteenth century. The theories that evolved openly reflected a hostile attitude toward homosexuality, based on little if any empirical evidence. Rather than challenge the historical rejection of homosexuality, these new views seemed determined to support it. Throughout the early decades of the nineteenth century, medical discussions of homosexuality were clearly imprinted with the bias of a more powerful religious tradition.

As time passed, homosexuality retained its pathological or disease status within the medical community. Whatever research was done centered around isolating the causes of homosexuality, without questioning the negative aspects attributed to it. This psychiatric evaluation of homosexuality remained essentially unchallenged until 1948, when a researcher named Alfred Kinsey published his extensive study of sexual behavior. Previously, the vast majority of studies on homosexuality had been primarily based on small numbers of patients gleaned from the private clinical practices of psychiatrists as well as from research done on homosexuals in prisons, mental hospitals, or the disciplinary barracks of the armed services. On the other hand, Kinsey's findings were drawn from an extraordinarily large group of Americans, reflecting a cross-section of the population.

The data, which spoke for itself, startled the American public. There appeared to be a tremendous variation between societal standards and what actually went on in bedrooms across the country. The study revealed that over 37 percent of the male population had engaged in sexual contact with another man on at least one occasion between adolescence and old age.

These results presented a challenge to orthodox psychiatric theory. If so many men engaged in both heterosexual and homosexual behavior throughout the course of their adult lives, could homosexuality still be regarded as a pathological illness? Kinsey and others believed that the statistical norm could not be psychologically abnormal. Kinsey concluded that the "capacity of an individual to respond erotically to any sort of stimulus . . . is basic to the species." He asserted that it was possible for an individual to have both hetero-sexual and homosexual responses.

Kinsey became extremely critical of the general trend of psychiatric research that centered on essen-tially searching for pathological or disturbed family backgrounds in homosexuals. He theorized instead that a complex variety of factors were involved in the determination of an individual's sexual orientation, and that sexual preference represented only one ex-ample of the "mysteries of human choice." He did not believe that it mattered whether an individual chose to meet his or her sexual needs with a member of the same sex or the opposite sex, but rather that problems only came into play through society's rejection of certain sexual practices and discrimination against those who practiced them.

Kinsey felt that neither biological nor psychological factors were responsible for the extensive predomi-nance of heterosexuality. He felt that sexual orienta-tion was instead learned by very young children early in life, and, in that sense, did not differ from other forms of societal behavior. Kinsey stressed that the culture tended to direct and guide the diffuse sexual drive of the very young, channelling it to meet socie-ty's "appropriate ends."

At a time when the overall psychiatric establish-ment was focused on trying to learn how an individual became homosexual, Kinsey instead pondered why more individuals did not act on their homosexual potential. He believed the answer lay in a heterosex-ual culture that discriminated against and was ex-tremely punitive toward homosexual behavior. In reaffirming heterosexuality as a medical norm to which psychotherapists felt obligated to help their homosexual patients conform, these doctors actually served to reinforce societal standards rather than deal specifically with the individual needs of their patients. Kinsey believed that there would be greater merit in psychotherapists assisting the vast variety of human beings to accept whatever sexual preference they felt most comfortable with.

Kinsey's research presented a genuine challenge to the psychiatric profession's views of homosexuality. A number of years later, the Institute for Sex Research, which Kinsey had established, engaged in further research on homosexual behavior. This served to substantiate Kinsey's original findings.

Three years after the initial publication of Kinsey's original investigation, some interesting results were published by two researchers named Cleland Ford and Frank Beach. Ford and Beach studied seventy-six cultures besides our own. In forty-nine of the societies studied, the researchers learned that some homosexual activity was considered normal and socially acceptable.

In several societies, certain male children were selectively reared to take on that role. In other instances, homosexual activity was regarded as a significant factor in the initiation rites engaged in at puberty by young boys. Homosexual behavior was often regarded as part of the normal behavior that characterized a young man's sexuality prior to his marriage. The overall conclusion of the Ford and Beach studies was that in some cultures homosexual activity was regarded as appropriate for all men during various times of their lives, and for a fairly small number of men who had been designated to fulfill a particular role within the given society, exclusive homosexual behavior was highly esteemed.

Ford and Beach also conducted research on the

sexual behavior of animals, which involved studying adult male monkeys. The researchers were attempting to determine if and to what extent the capacity for homosexual response existed in other species. The reports of their findings indicated that sexual activity between monkeys of the same sex did indeed occur. It was observed that at different times, some of the male monkeys engaged in both homosexual and heterosexual activity. Further research led Ford and Beach to conclude that an inherent biological tendency for homosexual responsiveness exists in all animal species.

These findings strongly challenged the argument that homosexuality was pathological because it was contrary to a fundamental biological drive. Ford and Beach resolved that the dominance of heterosexuality among human beings was the result of cultural forces:

> Men and women who are totally lacking in any conscious homosexual leanings are as much a product of cultural conditioning as are exclusive homosexuals who find heterosexual relations distasteful and unsatisfactory. Both extremes represent a movement away from the original indeterminant condition which includes the capacity for both forms of sexual expression.

Such conclusions furthered the drive to reevaluate the status classification of homosexuality as a psychological disorder. The evidence helped to undercut the claims of such a diagnosis as being value-free. If it were true that heterosexuality and homosexuality could both be determined culturally, then the question might shift to the science of human preferences.

The work of psychologist Evelyn Hooker during the

mid-1950s also served to point to the fact that homosexuality was not in and of itself a pathological condition. Dr. Hooker administered a series of psychological tests to a group of homosexuals and gave the same test series to a group of heterosexuals. She was anxious to find if the tests taken by the homosexual group revealed a greater level of pathology. The results showed that two-thirds of both the homosexual group and the heterosexual group were of average or better adjustment. It was impossible to find any differences between the two groups of individuals.

The work of Evelyn Hooker was acknowledged by her profession, and at the end of the 1960s she was selected to head the National Institute of Mental Health's Task Force on Homosexuality. The task force concluded that most of the suffering and hardships foisted on homosexuals were the result of discriminatory practices by a heterosexual society.

Another researcher whose work served to document that homosexuality was not an illness was Thomas Szaz. In the mid-1950s, Szaz published a number of critical essays that set forth the proposition that the psychiatric profession had taken over the function of socially and morally regulating society, a task that had been performed by religious institutions in the past. Szaz argued that moral value judgments should not be cloaked under the guise of medical authority. According to Szaz, "If moral values are to be discussed and promoted, they ought to be considered for what they are—moral values, not health values."

Szaz believed that heterosexuality was established as the recognized standard to insure that the biological requirements of reproduction be met. However, just because heterosexual behavior served to insure reproduction and the continuance of the species, this did not mean that homosexual behavior was immoral or a form of mental illness. He wrote: "We delude ourselves . . . if because of its biological value we accept heterosexuality as a social value. The jump from biological value to social value is the crux of human morality."

Szaz also warned against the dangers of psychiatrists' labeling homosexuality as a disease. He stressed the importance of recognizing and acknowledging that efforts to change an individual's sexual orientation through psychiatry was not a question of curing that person, but instead was a matter of changing that individual's values. Szaz felt that under these circumstances, it was essential for the therapist never to impose his or her own values under the guise of mental health, but to be certain to encourage the patient to reevaluate and choose what he or she really wants and feels most comfortable with.

Szaz wrote, "My contention that the psychiatric perspective on homosexuality is but a thinly disguised replica of the religious perspective which it displaced, and that its efforts to treat this kind of conduct medically are but thinly disguised methods of repressing it, may be verified by examining any contemporary psychiatric account of homosexuality."

Szaz went on to state that the "psychiatric preoccupation with the disease concept of homosexuality . . . conceals the fact that homosexuals are a group of medically stigmatized and socially persecuted individuals."

Still another critic of the traditional view of homosexuality as an illness was Judd Marnor, a well-known and respected psychiatrist. Marnor believed that sexuality was a product of learning, and as a result the expectations and demands of a society played a vital role in channelling an individual's sexuality. Marnor asserted that there was no such thing as a "homosexual personality." He felt that it might be extremely detrimental to develop assumptions about all homosexuals based upon the evidence from a relatively small number of homosexuals who had sought psychiatric care.

Like Szaz, Marnor perceived psychotherapists not as restoring homosexuals to good mental health, but rather simply helping them to adapt to the current cultural standards of the majority. He stated that the classification of homosexuality as a mental illness was an example of "society's aggressive intervention into the lives of individuals."

During the late 1960s and early 1970s, the psychiatric profession underwent a serious reevaluation of its classification of homosexuality. Ever-increasing evidence demonstrating that homosexuals were no more abnormal than heterosexuals. In addition, growing pressure from gay rights organizations called for a broader and fairer view of homosexuality.

Perhaps one of the most dramatic moments of this period occurred at the 1972 annual convention of the American Psychiatric Association. At that time, the plight of a hidden minority within the profession itself was brought to light. These were homosexual psychiatrists, many of whom were well respected within their field, but who had been forced to live with the fear of being found out and the possible subsequent ruin of their professional careers.

Calling himself Dr. Anonymous and wearing concealing clothing to obscure his identity, a gay psychiatrist addressed the panel. He informed the audience that at that very conference there were over two hundred homosexual psychiatrists in attendance. He also revealed that for some time there had been an underground association of gay psychoanalysts that held its own meetings at designated times during annual conventions of the American Psychiatric Association. Dr. Anonymous went on to state:

> As psychiatrists who are homosexual, we must know our place and what we must do to be successful. If our goal is high academic achievement, a level of earning capacity equivalent to our fellows, or admission to a psychoanalytic institute, we must make sure that we behave ourselves and that no one in a position of power is aware of our sexual preference and/or gender identity.
> Much like a black man with white skin who chooses to live as a white man, we can't be seen with our real friends, our real homosexual family, lest our secret be known and our doom sealed. . . . Those who are willing to speak openly will do so only if they have little to lose, and if you have little to lose, you won't be listened to.

As increasing numbers of psychiatrists began to shed their own unfounded prejudices, it became clear that significant changes regarding the classification of homosexuality were underway. In 1971 the San Francisco affiliate of the National Association of Mental Health adopted a resolution stating that "homosexuality can no longer be equated only with sickness, but may properly be considered as a preference, orientation, or propensity for certain kinds of life styles." In 1972, the Golden Gate chapter of the National Association of Social Workers enacted a similar resolution. An ever-growing number of psychiatrists were now anxious to see the classification of homosexuality as an illness deleted from the prominent diagnostic tool of the psychiatric profession, the Diagnostic and Statistical Manual.

All these events came to a climax at the 1973 annual American Psychiatric Convention. Commenting on the significance of the convention, *Newsweek* magazine stated, "The indication seems to be that the Committee will decide to drop homosexuality from its list of mental aberrations." Indeed, within days, homosexuality was deleted from the manual describing psychiatric disorders, and the organization issued a statement claiming that "homosexuality . . . by itself does not necessarily constitute a psychiatric disorder."

The American Psychiatric Association also went on record as being against the societal prejudice and discrimination against gays and lesbians and condemned the use of criminal sanctions against consenting adults engaging in homosexual behavior. The following statement was issued to the public by the committee:

Whereas homosexuality in and of itself implies no impairment in judgment, stability, reliability or vocational capacities, therefore, be it resolved that the American Psychiatric Association deplores all public and private discrimination against homosexuals in such areas as employment, housing, public accommodations, and licensing, and declares that no burden of proof of such judgment, capacity, or reliability shall be placed upon homosexuals greater than that imposed on any other persons.

Further, the APA supports and urges the enactment of civil rights legislation at local, state, and federal levels that would insure homosexual citizens the same protection now guaranteed to others. Further, the APA supports and urges the repeal of all legislation making criminal offenses of sexual acts performed by consenting adults in private.

The American Psychiatric Association's president issued a statement stating that he hoped that the Association's resolution would "help to build a more accommodative climate of opinion for the homosexual minority in our country, a climate which would enable homosexuals to render the maximal contribution to society of which they are capable."

News of the American Psychiatric Association's decision to declare that homosexuality could not be equated with mental illness headlined the front pages of major newspapers across America. The *New York Times* wrote, "Psychiatrists in a Shift. Declare Homosexuality No Mental Illness," while the *Washington Post* printed the words, "Doctors Rule Homosexuals Not Abnormal." Gay rights groups were jubilant; *The Advocate,* a gay newspaper, heralded the historic resolution with the words, "Sick No More."

CHAPTER EIGHT

Telling Parents and Family

"Mom, Dad, there's something I have to tell you—I'm a homosexual."

For many gays and lesbians, the above words are not spoken easily. Interviews with young gays and lesbians have borne out the fact that most homosexuals often feel more comfortable revealing their sexual orientation to their friends or siblings than to their parents.

Some gay and lesbian people believe this hesitancy may at least be partly due to the fact that for a great many young people, parents symbolically stand for authority within our societal structure. They are the ones most directly responsible for the proper socialization of their offspring, teaching the young child how to function effectively within the framework of everyday living.

Although it might not be the soundest attitude to take, many parents firmly believe that their offspring's attributes and performance reflect their own success or failure as parents. Often that child represents their last opportunity to attain goals they themselves never reached. Unfortunately, too often such aspirations are not in keeping with the child's own goals, abilities, or temperament.

The degree to which parents may be overly involved in their child's life style varies among families. Some parents effectively separate from their children and are able to acknowledge and respect their mature offspring as a young adult in his or her own right, worthy of their love and friendship. For them, the fact that their child's values may differ from their own is not as important as the young person's right to happiness and satisfaction.

Those may be ideal conditions under which to come of age. However, the actual experiences of most young people is different. Parental reactions to a young person's embarking on a dramatically different life choice will vary a great deal, depending on a number of factors. Among these are how the parents view the child's choice, how they feel about themselves as parents, and how willing they are to accept their grown offspring as a separate individual having the right to make his or her own decisions.

Ken, a twenty-year-old gay college student, describes his experience:

I knew that I was gay for about two or three years before I told my Mom and Dad about it. Looking back now, I don't think it was my apprehension about their reaction to it as much as my own need to come to grips with who I was. I had to learn to like and respect myself.

I felt very secure and happy in my life style by the time I approached my parents with the news. I was living in an off-campus apartment with a young man with whom I was very much in love. I wanted my parents to meet him and share some of the joy that this relationship had brought me.

Although I guess at first it felt a little awkward telling them, I honestly don't believe that I ever imagined my parents might not accept me. I somehow expected them to embrace my new life style with the same enthusiasm I was experiencing.

After all, hadn't I been brought up by a mother and father who had always appeared to be devout liberals on every frontier? When I was younger, I remember that my grandfather used to tease them, saying that they ought to make certain that there weren't any liberal causes out in the world that they'd missed. It had always been so important for my parents to voice their support for fairness and equality in any situation.

As a child, I remember being taken on peace marches and to civil rights demonstrations. My parents were always collecting signatures on petitions to be sent to Congress to either bring about nuclear disarmament or to clean up the environment. My mother worked as a social worker, while my Dad owned and operated a small community newspaper with a strong liberal bent. Whenever the topic of gay rights had come up, my parents had always expressed their disdain over the terrible prejudices and abuse homosexuals in our society are made to endure.

I had always thought of my mother as a brave, resourceful woman. In my entire life, I had never seen my mother cry. She had retained her composure even as she watched my little sister die of a rare blood disease. Yet when I revealed to her that

I was gay, she cried for nearly two-and-a-half days. My father slipped into a depressed state. For the entire evening after I told them, he kept dropping his head into his hands, and wondering aloud why this was happening to them. I tried to explain to my parents that nothing had happened to *them*, but rather that something wonderful had happened to me. I had found out who I really was, and I liked myself. To have their understanding and support, and to be able to honestly share my life with them, would even further enrich my existence. If I had to, I could forgo my relationship with my parents, but I cared for them both a great deal and wanted very much for them to continue to be in my life.

As things turned out, Ken did manage to maintain a good, ongoing relationship with both his father and mother. In time, they also came to accept and like his roommate. However, it's important to note that everything did not come together all at once. At first Ken's parents tended to blame themselves for their son's homosexuality. They reminded Ken that he would now be an easy target for the hostility of intolerant others. They said that they couldn't bear to see their only son suffer such indignities.

Ken took the time to reassure his parents that he was not suffering, but was in fact happier than he had ever been in his entire life. He felt secure and comfortable in his sexual orientation, and he had found a wonderful mate as well as a whole circle of intelligent and sociable gay friends. He was also currently working with a gay student activist group on his campus to help end discrimination against gays and lesbians. Ken felt his parents had provided him with an upbringing that had allowed him to like himself, have confidence in his own choices, and face his future with courage and enthusiasm. He didn't know how much his parents had to do with his homosexuality, or how much might be attributable to heredity or outside environmental influences. He was just glad that his parents had played some part in making him the whole person he had become, and he made certain his parents knew how he felt.

Within several months, Ken's parents managed to view and discuss pertinent issues in Ken's love life in very much the same way such incidents would be regarded if Ken had been heterosexual. They came to realize that, in reality, Ken hadn't changed. He was the same wonderful son they had always loved.

Ken's story had a happy ending, but this isn't always the case. When Vanessa, a nineteen-year-old word processor operator, told her parents that she was a lesbian, they refused to accept it. Vanessa's mother flew into a screaming rage, calling her daughter just about every unthinkable name possible. She blamed her daughter for "bringing this terrible shame on the family" and labeled Vanessa selfish and stupid. She said that she had already suspected for a number of years that Vanessa was "a bit weird," but she had never dreamed that her daughter would go this far.

Vanessa's father expressed extreme disappointment in his daughter. He said he had always thought of Vanessa as a good girl. He had believed that the reason Vanessa had not dated many men was due to the fact that she must have thought such encounters might eventually lead to sexual behavior that would conflict with her high standards of morality. He had believed that when Vanessa was ready for married life and children, she would find the right man and marry him.

Vanessa's father never imagined that his daughter had been spending her time loving other women.

Vanessa's parents agreed that Vanessa had destroyed their lives, as well as the life and future of her younger sister. They claimed that "no decent family" would want their son to marry their younger daughter once they found out that there was "perversion and insanity" in their family.

Vanessa's father and mother claimed that in her despicable choice, Vanessa had ruined their hope of ever enjoying Vanessa's children, who would have been their first grandchildren. They felt that the only legacy Vanessa had left to her family was shame.

After only a day or two of contemplation, Vanessa's parents elected to disown her. They felt that they couldn't tolerate such a willful, destructive daughter in their midst, and that it was their responsibility to keep Vanessa away from her younger sister. They expressed to Vanessa how important this separation from her younger sister was to them, as they firmly felt that any further association could damage her sister's reputation and marriage prospects. They also wanted to be certain that Vanessa did not have an opportunity to influence her little sister with what they regarded as her degenerate thinking.

Vanessa could hardly believe the lengths to which her parents were prepared to go to cast her out of the family. When Vanessa's mother found a letter from Vanessa to her younger sister and realized that the two sisters had been writing to one another secretly, she threatened to disown her younger daughter as well if the correspondence between them continued.

This was extremely difficult for the younger girl, who viewed her sister as an innocent victim of their parents' prejudice and wished to remain as close to her older sister as she had always been. However, their parents' determination in this matter was so strong that Vanessa's younger sister lacked the courage to stand up for Vanessa's actions. She believed that openly defending Vanessa at this point would only jeopardize her own relationship with her parents. She also felt that taking Vanessa's side would do nothing to bring Vanessa back into her parents' good graces; they would only think that Vanessa had corrupted her as well. At this point in her life, Vanessa's younger sister felt torn between her feelings for Vanessa and her loyalty to her parents.

As months passed, Vanessa did what she could to help heal the rift that now existed between her parents and herself. She sent her parents an anniversary card, to which there was no reply. She sent her mother a birthday gift—something she knew her mother had wanted for a long time—but the gift was returned without a note.

However, Vanessa still loved and missed her family and felt that she didn't want to be permanently separated from them. She was certain that much of their reaction stemmed from shock, fear, and a great deal of misinformation about what gays and lesbians were really like. Vanessa believed that as people, homosexuals were not any different from her parents, but she knew that her mother and father didn't know this. Vanessa wanted her parents to know that she hadn't changed; she was still the loving and decent daughter they had raised.

Traditionally, her family had always spent Christmas Eve together in a festive holiday celebration. After enjoying a hearty turkey dinner, they would decorate the Christmas tree and exchange gifts. So at just about the time her family would be starting their meal, Vanessa arrived at the door armed with gifts for everyone. She hoped that the Christmas spirit would aid her in this effort to become reunited with her family.

Vanessa rang the bell and anxiously waited to see who would answer the door. It was her father, and at the sight of Vanessa standing in the doorway, he flew into a rage before even giving his daughter an opportunity to speak. His face flushed red, and with the veins jutting out of his forehead, he screamed at Vanessa, "It wasn't enough that you disgraced our whole family, now you have to ruin whatever we have left of a holiday too."

At that point he seemed to lose control. He struck Vanessa hard across the face. The blow was so forceful that Vanessa was knocked to the ground. Her father looked at her and then stared down at his hand as if in disbelief. "God help me," he said, "I never hit a woman in my life." Regaining his composure, he added, "But you're not a real woman, are you? I don't know what you are, but you're not my daughter anymore, I'll tell you that for certain."

With those words her father turned and walked into the house, without even trying to help his daughter to her feet. Vanessa heard her younger sister ask who was at the door. Their father answered simply, "Nobody."

Fortunately, Vanessa was not physically injured by the blow. She got up and walked home to her apartment, prepared to spend the remainder of the Christmas holiday with Annie, the young woman with whom she had been living for the past six months.

She later related to Annie that she felt as though her spirit had been crushed. She said she missed having parents in her life, but felt that her parents' blind prejudice had caused them to miss out on the joy of having a daughter as well. After what had happened on Christmas Eve, Vanessa was no longer prepared to accept any more of their physical or emotional abuse. She was willing to patch things up between her parents and herself, but now it was their turn to make the first move. Unfortunately, at the time of this writing, Vanessa's parents had not contacted her.

Perhaps Vanessa's story is a rather extreme example of what can happen when the views of parents and offspring collide on what is to be regarded as an acceptable sexual orientation. Although in many instances, parents have registered some degree of surprise and/or disappointment in learning of their child's homosexuality, in some situations parents as well as other family members have proved to be extremely supportive and helpful. Harriet, the mother of a twenty-year-old gay college student, explained:

When my son Michael first told me that he was gay, I wanted to die. Not because I was ashamed of Michael or anything like that. It was just that I learned my son had known for certain that he was gay from the time he was fourteen years old, and throughout that entire period Michael felt that he had to keep his feelings a secret.

I love my son and that will never change. I don't care whom he chooses as a mate. I'd just like to see Michael find someone who will be good to him. The primary concern should be finding a kind and responsible partner to share your life with, and as far as I'm concerned, that person's gender is secondary.

Michael told me he hid the fact that he was gay from me because he feared I'd be disappointed in him. I'm not disappointed in my son. He's a wonderful boy, he always has been, and I'm sure that if he wishes to love a man rather than a woman, then that must be what's right for him. I'm only disappointed in myself for not sufficiently conveying to him that he could never lose my love for choosing to lead his life in a way that differed from how I lead mine.

I shudder to think of what Michael must have gone through and how he had to endure it all alone. He recently told me how he was beaten up twice by a gang of roughnecks in high school, and tormented through an entire summer at camp. He was too ashamed and hurt to confide in anyone, so none of us ever had the opportunity to comfort him through those difficult times.

Now Michael has changed. He's turned into a happy and confident young man, and although he's a member of a very much discriminated-against minority group, he and his friends are actively working with gay rights groups to turn that around.

I'm doing my best to help as well. I've participated in protest marches and political rallies for gay rights. I've worked with gay parents' groups as well as with gay rights political lobbying caucuses in an attempt to have legislation passed to help end discrimination against homosexuals.

I'm glad that Michael is my son, and I'm proud of him in every way. Now I intend to put a good deal of my energy toward helping to create a more tolerant society for all of us to live in.

* * *

Telling Parents and Family

By the time a young person is ready to confront his or her parents with the fact that he or she is a homosexual, that individual may feel fairly comfortable with his or her own sexual preference. However, the parents who are hearing the news for the first time may not be as sophisticated or knowledgeable about homosexuality, and as a result may feel ashamed or reluctant to seek help, support, or advice from trusted friends, counselors, or clergy. In such instances, parents find themselves in a position in which they are expected to be ready and willing to offer help and encouragement to their offspring, while in reality they may be in dire need of just this sort of support themselves. Many may be too embarrassed and upset to tell anyone.

In interviews with parents of gays and lesbians, the feeling most commonly shared by them on first learning of their child's homosexuality was guilt. Often parents will mentally go back over the young person's entire life trying to understand how they failed as parents.

At times, parents may firmly decide that they are responsible for their offspring's homosexuality. It may seem almost as if they are searching for areas in their child's upbringing where they might have failed. As one mother put it, "If only I had put a stop to Jenny being a tomboy, then everything would have probably turned out all right. If I had insisted that she wear dresses with ruffles and attend the school dances, then I might have been able to prevent this whole terrible thing."

It's also not uncommon to hear fathers unjustly blame themselves for their son's homosexuality, claiming that if only they had played ball with the boy more often, he would have probably turned out to be heterosexual. Although there is no scientific evidence to support these conclusions, they may continue to exist in the parent's mind all the same.

Sometimes such feelings of guilt may erupt into angry, defensive accusations such as, "How could you have turned out this way? I always did right by you," or "It was the sick friends you always hung around with that made you this way. I certainly had nothing to do with it."

Although such reactions may be distressing to the young gay or lesbian individual, it is important to remember that behind the apparent anger, the parent may be experiencing a great deal of pain too.

Often the parents will hurt for both the child and themselves. Having grown up in a society that is extremely antihomosexual, parents have a good idea of what the offspring they loved and nurtured all these years will have to endure. The screaming, the accusations, the name-calling, and blame-placing that may occur are all often little more than futile attempts at dealing with the painful reality that their child is not going to have an easy time of it, and, as a result, neither are they.

It isn't always easy for parents who have long dreamed of a traditional life for their child to accept that their offspring is going to be different. Sometimes this revelation may feel like a personal affront to unsuspecting parents who are most comfortable with their own acceptance of and conformity to societal norms. However, parents who base their actions on these feelings, and persist in destructive and accusatory behavior, are not accomplishing anything useful or constructive for their child or for the family as a whole. As Hilda, a fifty-eight-year-old mother, expressed it:

> When I initially learned that my son was gay, I was upset. But, at the same time, I knew that I still loved my boy and wanted him in my life. I felt that now I had to be extremely careful not to say anything that might devastate my son and drive him away from our family permanently. I tried to concentrate on the positives. I kept asking myself questions like, What would be the best way to respond to my son, and how can I possibly be of real help to him? Where can I find accurate information on homosexuality, so that I can better understand the situation? Where can I go for counseling so that I can learn how to best cope with my own feelings about having a gay son? I tried to follow a sensible path of action in the hope that an attitude of this nature would be most beneficial to my son at this point in his life and would assist in mending our family.

A father spoke of accepting his lesbian daughter in this manner:

> At first I kept hoping that my daughter Abbie would change. Of course, it just didn't happen, but I still continuously tried to get her to see psychotherapists, because initially I kept viewing her homosexuality as an illness and I was in search of a cure. I continued to think that if she were only shown by a professional that she had somehow taken a wrong turn, then she might rethink what she had become.

Abbie didn't want to disappoint me. She said that she did want to be more in the mainstream because she knew that then there would be fewer problems. However, these attempts were anything but successful. Abbie became extremely despondent and depressed after several months of trying to become heterosexual through therapy. She said that it wasn't working and what she really needed was to learn to accept herself as she really was. Eventually, my daughter came to do just that.

I've now learned that the medical profession no longer regards homosexuality as a sickness, but rather as another life choice. It was important for me also to stop trying to make Abbie what I wanted her to be and learn instead to love and accept her for herself. It turned out not to be my daughter who had to outgrow her homosexuality, but rather I who came to outgrow my need to insist that she develop a heterosexual orientation.

Still another mother spoke of her lesbian daughter in this manner:

At first it was so hard for me to believe that my daughter Kristin was a lesbian, because she simply never looked the way I thought all lesbians had to look. She never wore a short mannish haircut or dressed in a masculine or even tailored fashion. Kristin was a young woman who loved long curls and lots of frills. Pink had been her favorite color since childhood. She had always insisted that her room be pink and many of her clothes were pink.

Kristin has now explained to me that I had

formerly only thought of lesbians stereotypically. After meeting a number of my daughter's friends, I've seen that all lesbians do not wear mannish suits and orthopedic shoes. Some look as traditionally feminine as my daughter; others seem to be quite in keeping with current fashion trends. I've learned that gay and lesbian individuals are not any more mass produced than are heterosexuals, and that within any grouping of people there is an enormous range of variation. There are many thousands of gays and lesbians who appear to be so much like their heterosexual colleagues and casual acquaintances that they are often believed to be heterosexual as well. I've discarded my outmoded attitudes, and I feel it's important for everyone to realize just how limiting stereotyped views of other human beings can be.

It is extremely important to many gays and lesbians to be able to share meaningful events and relationships in their lives with their parents and family. Too often a great deal of energy that could be channeled constructively is used in devising elaborate tales to perpetuate hiding the truth. As a result, the barriers between parent and child are only further solidified.

Many young gays and lesbians have expressed the belief that much unnecessary unhappiness has been generated by parents who have persisted in remaining unyielding and critical. They feel that the parents who eventually find it easiest to deal with having a homosexual offspring are those who are willing to sit down with their child and really listen to what he or she has to say despite what their own feelings might be. Parents who realize that they may need to learn more about homosexuality and must perhaps reevaluate old thinking are usually best prepared to pursue a positive course of action in keeping their families together. Naturally, this realization may not come all at once to even the most liberal of parents. Often it takes some time and understanding on both sides.

For gay and lesbian individuals, there is really no single best way to tell their parents that they are homosexual. Although they may hope their parents will accept the news with an open and relaxed attitude, this is not always going to be so. Although it may be impossible to insist that parents accept that which they feel compelled to refute, some homosexual counselors have found the following to be helpful in the initial discussion:

1. An individual's own attitude about himself or herself, as well as how that person feels about homosexuality generally, is important in relating his or her sexual orientation to others. It is always easier to like and accept people who feel comfortable with themselves. Some counselors believe that if gay or lesbian individuals feel particularly good about themselves at this point in their lives, then it is important for them to convey this feeling to their parents in the discussion. If part of the parental concern stems from the belief that being homosexual will make their child neurotic or unhappy when in fact the child is not, their offspring may serve as living proof that this need not be the case.

2. Timing is extremely crucial in sensitive matters. Many counselors do not believe it wise for homosexuals to reveal their sexual orientation to their parents during an argument, as parents may perceive this as a weapon used to hurt them. In any case, it is important for the parents not to feel that they may justifiably strike back at their child for hurting them.

Telling Parents and Family

In choosing a time and place to discuss this with parents, it might be best to consider whatever else is happening within the family at the time. It is important that the disclosure not add to other new or unsettling events that may be taking a toll on the parents' emotional resources.

3. Some counselors believe that whether or not both parents should be told at the same time will usually depend on the particular situation. If the offspring feels that one parent may be more sympathetic than the other, it might be wisest to first confide in that individual. Often an understanding parent can become an important ally in winning the other over. However, if either parent is at all competitive, it is important to avoid playing one parent against the other in any way.

When telling parents, it is essential for the individual to reassure them that he or she loves them and always wishes to remain their son or daughter. At times, homosexual counselors have suggested that it may be best to stress that the love a person feels for a member of his or her own sex need not stand in the way of the special bond shared between parent and child. Parents should be reminded that they liked their son or daughter well enough yesterday, and that their offspring is still the same person. All the same positive qualities exist. Individuals who find it awkward to discuss love in this manner with their parents should try using the word "feelings" instead.

Most parents grew up in a society that discriminated against homosexuals. When they initially hear the news, all the negative stereotypes accumulated over a lifetime may spring to mind. Counselors have stressed that to really understand who their child is, these parents may have to work through a good deal of misinformation. Changing the dream of what their child's future may hold may not come easily. It is important to allow them time, and to encourage communication between family members.

4. Some homosexual counselors have affirmed that in most instances, it is not a good idea for the lover to accompany the son or daughter when his or her sexual orientation is revealed to the parents. If a nonfamily member is present, the parents may not feel as free to ask questions or speak as openly as they might if alone with their child.

If an individual feels that it is essential to bring along his or her lover for emotional support, that person should carefully consider the advantages of doing so against the potential consequences. For most parents, it is easier to first come to terms with the concept of their child's homosexuality before meeting the person with whom their offspring is romantically involved.

5. Perhaps the most difficult possibility to deal with is that even if an individual does all of the above and more, the parents may still lash out at or reject him or her. However, this may be their initial reaction. In such instances, it is important to remember that making the decision to reveal one's sexual orientation to one's parents is often the culmination of a lengthy personal growth process. Newly informed parents are just beginning that process themselves. Counselors stress the importance of keeping the lines of communication open, and suggest trying to find ways of introducing books, articles, discussion groups, or documentary films to the family that may serve to inform and enlighten. In instances in which everyone has been willing, some gay and lesbian individuals have found it helpful to introduce to their families some of their homosexual friends who defy the com-

mon stereotypes. Many parents have found it helpful to speak to a professional therapist or counselor who has an understanding and supportive attitude toward homosexuality.

6. Many gay and lesbian counselors have stated that throughout the entire disclosure process it is essential to keep in mind and stress to the parents that a strong and united family is something that everyone wants and should be willing to work for together.

In some areas there are peer support groups to help families adjust to having a gay member. One such group, known as Parents of Gays (POG), exists in a number of states throughout the country. Numerous other groups, both formal and informal, have arisen as well. Many gay and lesbian organizations have a special task force or committee to deal with such issues.

Timing and patience are usually extremely crucial elements when dealing with such matters. As one mother said, "When I learned that my son was gay, I felt as though I didn't want him to be my child any longer. But I still loved him, and I just couldn't crush that feeling and keep it hidden inside of me forever. After a time, I came to want him near me again, and to be as proud of him as I was before I knew that he was a homosexual. It can happen. It happened to me."

CHAPTER NINE

The AIDS Crisis

Brian was twenty-one years old and a senior at a well-known university in the East when he realized that he seemed unable to get rid of a bad cold that had continued for most of the winter. He always felt tired and frequently broke out in a sweat during the night. Although Brian developed a persistent cough, he failed to seek medical attention, since he believed there was nothing seriously wrong with him.

He blamed his drop in weight and swollen lymph glands on being overtired. Brian had taken on a hectic spring academic schedule, but even after dropping two courses and allowing for more relaxation time, Brian found that he was still experiencing headaches and at times ran a fever. When he broke out in a purplish skin rash on his face and along the left side of his neck, he saw a doctor at the university's health service.

Brian was diagnosed as having AIDS. Eighteen months later, he was dead.

Acquired Immune Deficiency Syndrome (AIDS) is a breakdown in the body's immune system. The immune system is the mechanism by which the body combats diseases and infections. When the system doesn't function properly, the body is left vulnerable to unusual infections and other illnesses. Many of these illnesses can be life-threatening. Few people have lived longer than two years after being diagnosed as AIDS sufferers.

Among the illnesses that most commonly afflict AIDS victims is a group known as "opportunistic infections." Some of these opportunistic infections are Pneumocystis carinii pneumonia, chronic cytomegalovirus (CMV), unusually severe shingles and herpes simplex, and certain bacteria (including one that causes a form of tuberculosis). Kaposi's sarcoma, a form of skin cancer, has also been associated with AIDS.

Not a great deal is known about AIDS. Significantly more research needs to be done in order to gain the much-needed insight into this still-baffling illness. Recently, Dr. Robert Gallo of the National Cancer Institute identified the cause of AIDS as a virus variant called HTLV-3. Similar findings were reported by the Pasteur Institute in Paris, where the virus was named LAV (lymphademopathy-associated virus). It is now believed that HTLV-3 and LAV are identical. Advances underway as a result of this discovery are a test that will identify the AIDS virus in blood supplies as well as a vaccine to prevent the disease.

In recent years AIDS has swept across the country in epidemic proportions. So far, AIDS victims have fallen into several distinguishable groups, with a high number of cases reported nationally among gay and bisexual men. Other groups have included intravenous drug users, Haitian immigrants, and hemophiliacs. In addition, there is very recent evidence to suggest the spread of AIDS among the heterosexual population as well. However, initially, over 90 percent of the earliest diagnosed AIDS cases were among gay and bisexual men. (There has not been a significant number of AIDS cases among lesbians.)

Many symptoms of AIDS are similar to those of other common illnesses. Therefore, it is important for a gay individual not to panic if he has experienced one or more of the symptoms listed below. However, it is especially important for homosexual men to recognize the early warning signs and seek medical attention immediately if two or more of these symptoms persist. Among the most common early symptoms of AIDS are:

Feelings of exhaustion and fatigue
Night sweats, fevers and chills, episodes of shaking and weakness
Weight loss unrelated to diet
Swollen glands or enlarged lymph nodes persisting for over two weeks
A purplish rash that is usually painless
Persistent sore throat
Persistent heavy cough
Appearance of white spots in mouth
Persistent diarrhea
Tendency to bruise easily
Severe headaches
Blurred vision

With the advent of the AIDS epidemic, gay groups across the nation have rallied to the support of AIDS victims. Preventive guidelines and other supportive materials have been made available to the general public. The New York Physicians for Human Rights have compiled the following AIDS Risk Reduction Guidelines distributed by the Gay Men's Health Crisis:

Know your partner, his state of health, his life style, and how many different sexual partners he has. . . . The fewer partners, the less your risk of acquiring the disease.
Engage in sex in a setting that is conducive to good hygiene. (Shower before and after sex)
Exchanging certain body fluids has a higher risk of transmitting diseases.
Urinating after sex may reduce your risk of acquiring some infections.
Eliminate the use of all street drugs, alcohol, and marijuana, as studies have shown these may impair the body's immune system and your judgment.
Maintain your body's immune system by eating well, exercising, and getting adequate rest. Cope with stress by learning relaxation techniques. See your physician regularly.

A number of gay and lesbian counselors have suggested the following for friends and family members of individuals stricken with AIDS:

1. Do not attempt to avoid the AIDS victim. Act as the friend or loved one you have always been.
2. Offer to assist with household chores and shopping. However, be certain not to undermine the individual's remaining strength by trying to take over

duties of which he is still capable and wishes to do himself. Always ask before doing anything.
3. Discuss the future with him as well as current events. Try not to allow him to feel that the world has passed him by.
4. If he wants to discuss his illness with you, allow him to do so. Listen carefully to his feelings and bring a positive, supportive attitude to the conversation. Your reaction may mean more to him than you realize.

Further information on AIDS is available at the following resource centers:

PHILADELPHIA AIDS TASK FORCE HOTLINE
(215) 232-8055
Call Sunday, Monday, or Wednesday, 7P.M. to 11P.M.;
Friday, 9 P.M. to 11P.M., Saturday, 9A.M. to 12 noon.

NATIONAL GAY TASK FORCE AIDS INFORMATION
1-800-221-7044 toll-free
3 P.M. to 9 P.M. daily

AIDS/KS FOUNDATION (San Francisco Area)
(415) 864-4373

AIDS Action Committee
Fenway Community Health Center
16 Haviland Street
Boston, Massachusetts 02115 (617) 267-7573

The AIDS Action Line (Boston)
(617) 536-7733
Monday-Friday, 11 A.M.to 6 P.M.

AIDS Project/Los Angeles
937 North Cole Avenue
Los Angeles, California 90038 (213) 871-1284
from southern California, call the toll-free AIDS
Hotline 1-800-922-AIDS

Gay Men's Health Crisis
Box 274
132 West 24th Street
New York, New York 10011 (212) 807-6655

CHAPTER TEN

Homosexuality
and the Law

Over the years, gay and lesbian individuals have been discriminated against in employment, the military, housing, the right to marry, child custody, student organizations, and many other areas. However, the past decade or so has witnessed an increased effort by homosexuals—and by heterosexuals who support their quest for equality—to place the issues before the courts and legislatures.

The emphasis of these efforts has been that gays and lesbians are human beings as well as United States citizens. As such, they are entitled to the protection and benefit of the law and are fully protected in the exercise of their constitutional rights.

Perhaps some of the earliest cases of unlawful discrimination against homosexuals that were tried before the courts involved the right of homosexual public employees to retain their positions unless and until their homosexuality in some way hampered their ability to perform their duties. One such case was *Morrison* v. *State Board of Education*. It was decided in 1969 by the California Supreme Court. Morrison, an outstanding schoolteacher with numerous years of classroom experience, had continued in his career successfully until 1964 when it was reported to his district's superintendent that Morrison had been involved in a homosexual affair. In May of that year, Morrison resigned. The vast majority of such cases usually ended in that manner. Many gay and lesbian teachers found it too much of a personal hardship to take the issue further. Going to court meant focusing a public spotlight on something as private as their sexuality, and most individuals were not willing to deal with the publicity and consequences that usually followed. It was easier to move to another town where they were not known.

Unfortunately for Morrison, however, the incident was not laid to rest even after he resigned. On August 5, 1965, an action was filed with the California State Board of Education to have Morrison's teacher's license revoked. If this action went through, Morrison would be prohibited from employment in any public school in the state of California. In March of the following year, the board did revoke his California teaching license, "because of immoral and unprofessional conduct and acts involving moral turpitude." Subsequently, Morrison took his case to court.

Morrison was victorious in the court battle. The court ruled that a teacher could only be discharged if his conduct adversely affected his ability to teach, and thereby rendered his job performance unsatisfactory. Being a homosexual was not sufficient cause for dismissal; Morrison had always been thought of as an exemplary teacher.

The California Supreme Court ruled that Morrison's teaching credentials should be immediately restored to him. The court stated, "In determining whether the teacher's conduct thus indicates unfitness to teach, the board may consider such matters as the likelihood that the conduct may have adversely affected students or fellow teachers, the degree of such adversity anticipated, the proximity or remoteness in time of the conduct, the type of teaching certificate held by the party involved, the praiseworthiness or blameworthiness of the motives resulting in the conduct, the likelihood of the recurrence of the questioned conduct, and the extent to which disciplinary action may inflict an adverse impact or chilling effect upon the constitutional rights of the teacher involved or other teachers."

Although Morrison was successful in his court battle, not all gays and lesbians in similar situations have fared as well. Some courts still reflect societal prejudices that in some instances have interfered with the dispensing of justice and with the constitutional rights of gays and lesbians.

Another area in which gays and lesbians have taken an important issue to the courts involves the right of homosexual student groups to be recognized on college and university campuses. When a college or university refuses to recognize a student organization, that group often may be denied the right to use campus facilities available to other groups as well as be denied the funding granted to similar campus organizations.

When initially applying for recognition as a campus student group, Gay Lib was flatly turned down by the University of Missouri. The university president stated, "The organization of Gay Lib, by applying for recognition, is attempting to obtain the tacit approval of homosexuality by the University of Missouri. Homosexuality is generally treated in the state of Missouri as being a socially repugnant concept." The university's board of trustees echoed the sentiments.

When the case was first heard, the district court upheld the position of the university. However, when the decision was appealed, the Eighth Circuit Court of Appeals reversed the decision in favor of the Gay Lib group. The court decision included the following remarks: "There is absolutely no evidence that the appellants intend to violate any state law or regulation of the University or even that they will advocate such violations. . . . the ancient halls of learning will survive even the most offensive verbal assaults upon traditional moral values; solutions to tough problems are never found in the repression of ideas."

The court ordered the University of Missouri to grant Gay Lib full recognition as a student campus organization, and also determined that the university pay the legal fees incurred by Gay Lib for having had to bring the case to court.

A similar incident took place in Virginia. The Gay Alliance for Students won full recognition and privileges as an official campus organization at Virginia Commonwealth University after appealing before the Fourth Circuit Court of Appeals. The court stated the following in response to what it regarded as an attempt at repression by the university: "It rings the death knell of a free society. . . . once used to stifle the thought that we hate, it can stifle ideas we love. It signals a lack of faith in people, in its supposition that they are unable to choose in the marketplace of ideas."

The right to act as a faculty advisor to a gay student campus group without the penalty of job termination was won in 1977 by Richard Aumiller through a decision of the U.S. District Court of Delaware. Aumiller, a theater arts instructor at the University of Delaware, had accepted the offer to serve as faculty advisor to a university group known as the Gay Community.

When the university refused to renew Aumiller's teaching contract at the appropriate time, Aumiller sued the University of Delaware in court and won. The court stated that Aumiller did not intentionally or recklessly attempt to create the false impression that he was acting as a university spokesman, "and as a result there were no grounds for his dismissal." Since the University of Delaware had infringed on the teacher's First Amendment rights, the court awarded Aumiller the year's salary lost while the case went to court as well as $10,000 in compensation for the mental distress he was made to suffer. The university was further ordered to delete any mention of the incident from the teacher's personnel file.

In recent years, numerous cases similar to the ones described here have been fought and won in court. Many gay student groups are now fully recognized on campuses across America.

Court battles have been won as well by gay high school students in pursuit of their rights. The Rhode Island Federal District Court affirmed the right of a gay male student to bring a male as his date to the high school prom.

Other gay organizations have gone to court in an effort to secure their right to public forum. The Alaska Gay Coalition waged a court battle when the mayor of the city of Anchorage removed a description of their group from the 1976-77 Anchorage Blue Book, a directory of service organizations in the Anchorage area. Because the Blue Book was financed by the city, the initial trial upheld the mayor's right to remove the organization from the listing. However, this decision was reversed by the Supreme Court, which stated, "The Blue Book was clearly an appropriate place for the communication of the type of information submitted by the Gay Coalition . . . [it] was designed for and dedicated to expressive and associational use and therefore once it was open for such use, the government could not deny [the Alaska Gay Coalition] access to it based solely on the content of its belief."

Although court battles have been won in various areas to end discrimination against gay and lesbian individuals, their struggle for full equality has been far from realized.

Until the early 1960s, sexual acts between persons of the same sex were illegal in every state. These laws, which were usually only selectively enforced, were often employed as harassment techniques against homosexuals. Discrimination of this nature forced many gays and lesbians to live out important parts of their lives secretly.

Today, sexual acts between consenting adults has been decriminalized in twenty-seven states. However, that still means that in over half of the states in the union, homosexual behavior remains technically illegal. Often such criminal acts are as vaguely defined as "gross indecencies between two men" or "gross indecencies between two women." Violations may carry penalties of more than fifteen years in prison.

There are also few laws to help prevent discrimination against gays and lesbians in the area of employment. An employer in private industry is free to hire whomever he or she wishes. The only federal law that restricts private industry employment practices is Title VII of the Civil Rights Act of 1964. This forbids discrimination against a candidate seeking employment on the basis of sex or race. Although this law protects women and racial minorities, it does not protect homosexuals from employment discrimination. No federal or state legislation exists that protects gay and lesbian workers in private industry from being fired for no cause other than the personal biases of their employers.

Some recent minor changes may help to end employment discrimination against gays and lesbians. Gay rights groups in several areas have secured policy statements from major private corporations that ensure that homosexual workers and job applicants will in no way be discriminated against by these corporations. In addition, some towns, boroughs, and counties have passed ordinances to prevent discrimination against gays and lesbians in private industry.

Public employment practices differ somewhat, as federal and state governments are not permitted to fire an employee without due process of law. However, the military is not covered by any regulations of this sort, and over the years numerous military personnel who were found to be homosexuals were forced to leave the military with dishonorable discharges. In fact, the Defense Department has issued strict regulations banning homosexuals from the military.

Still another area in which gays and lesbians are discriminated against involves the area of matrimony. Homosexuals are not permitted to marry one another, and as a result gay and lesbian couples are denied this special legal status and all the extending privileges reserved for their heterosexual counterparts.

Married people enjoy numerous legal and economic advantages denied to unmarried couples living together. In most states, married people are usually entitled to special tax and survivor benefits. In addition, insurance companies devise advantageous medical and property insurance programs for married people. These are unavailable to individuals who reside together and consider themselves a family. Survivor pension benefits are often only available to a legal spouse.

Marriage in our society also bestows a special social status that symbolizes stability, maturity, and commitment. It is a status denied to coupled gays and lesbians who are deeply committed to their partners and wish to spend the duration of their lives together.

Gays and lesbians have also faced discrimination in the area of immigration. It is extremely difficult for a homosexual to enter the United States for the purpose of becoming a citizen, as gays and lesbians have automatically been denied the right to immigrate. Although such individuals may be of sound mind and of high moral character, they may be systematically excluded under the present immigration laws as sexual psychopaths. An alien who has been admitted to the United States can have his or her visa revoked if that individual is discovered to be homosexual.

Gay and lesbian individuals are discriminated against in the areas described here for no reason other than the fact that they are homosexual. The fact that they may be model citizens, neighbors, employees, or friends may be disregarded when it is revealed that they love someone of their own sex. In some situations, there is little legal recourse available to them. In instances where justice might be obtained in court, the individual must be prepared and willing to spend the time and money, and to bear the invasion of privacy that a legal battle of this nature may entail. The scales of justice do not always balance easily.

On a broader level, in recent years many gays and

lesbians have banded together to form political organizations. The overall effect of this has been the development of a gay rights movement.

Some homosexuals trace the birth of the gay rights movement to June 27, 1969, when police in New York City raided the Stonewall Inn, a bar in the heart of New York City's Greenwich Village gay community. Some who were present recall the raid as the final straw in a harassment campaign against gays and lesbians that had been fervently waged by the New York City police department. Angered patrons of the bar battled police in a riot that lasted several hours.

Today a national gay lobby and a gay political action committee have offices in Washington, D.C. The Gay Rights National Lobby, whose central purpose is to promote the passage of gay rights legislation, has been extremely successful in helping to obtain congressional approval for $47 million in funding for AIDS research. The group also helped to successfully block several bills introduced into Congress that contained antihomosexual provisions.

Other homosexual groups, such as the Gay Activists Alliance and the National Gay Task Force, have used both protest demonstrations and persistent lobbying in efforts to end discrimination against gays and lesbians. There have been some successes. Numerous cities and towns—among them Ann Arbor and East Lansing, Michigan; Los Angeles; Chicago; Detroit; San Francisco; and Washington, D.C.—have passed laws prohibiting discrimination against gays and lesbians in public accommodations, housing, education, real estate practices, and credit practices. In 1982, Wisconsin became the first state in the union to enact a gay rights law. In addition, executive orders or civil service rules guarantee some gay rights in California, Illinois, Michigan, New York, Ohio, and Pennsylvania.

Gays and lesbians have become active in both the Democratic and Republican parties, and a number of homosexual men and women have recently been elected to local and state offices.

CHAPTER ELEVEN

Young Gay and Lesbian Voices: Terri

"Being a sixteen-year-old lesbian leaves you in an impossible predicament. I don't know any other lesbians my own age, and none of the older women will go near me. It's like being caught between a rock and a hard place, and it has left me feeling more alone and apart from other people than anyone could possibly imagine.

"It seems as if I've always been drawn to other women. Until last summer, I had never really acted on my feelings. There was no one to whom I could confide about what was going on inside of me, and it just wasn't the kind of feeling that you let be known at school. It was only last summer when I got a job as a junior counselor at a summer camp in New Hampshire that I met and came to love Robin.

"Robin was the head counselor. She was nineteen, bright, funny, and kind—especially so to me. It was my first summer as an assistant camp counselor, and there was a lot I had to learn. Robin dealt lovingly and patiently with me through everything, including the time I nearly destroyed the papier mâché creations in our crafts workshop.

"Robin and I spent a good deal of time together. We were best friends before we were lovers. Then one evening while we were taking a swim in the lake alone at sunset, we just started fooling around and splashing one another. I ended up in Robin's arms. She held my head gently, covering my face with little kisses. That's how the most wonderful summer of my life began.

"Unfortunately, everything ended when summer camp came to a close in September. Robin remained in New Hampshire, where she lived, and I went back to resume my life in New Jersey with my parents. Robin and I corresponded for a few months, but after a time Robin stopped writing. I didn't really hold it against her; it's hard to keep up a long-distance romance when there's little hope of seeing the other person very often.

"After the summer with Robin, I was no longer content just to stay home hiding in my cocoon, waiting for something to happen. I felt that I could better cope now with being who I was, and I wanted a relationship. Like everybody else, I wanted love to be a part of my life.

"However, it hasn't been easy. I came across a gay/ lesbian newspaper that listed lesbian social groups and political organizations. I've even managed to attend several meetings, without my parents' knowledge. The women there are nice and they've included me on some of the organizational committees. But I can't help feeling that they regard me as a child. They're encouraging and supportive, yet manage to romantically maintain their distance. I feel more mothered than loved by them, and I am always conscious of the fact that at this time they are forced to view me primarily as an underaged girl.

"So until I can find another Robin (if another does indeed exist), I'm by myself. I've heard gay guys complain about how difficult it is to be homosexual in America and women cite the special problems of lesbians, but to me it all pales when I think about what a lesbian or gay teenager living in a small town goes through. I know, because I'm living with this loneliness every day of my life."

BIBLIOGRAPHY

Altman, Dennis. *The Homosexualization of America: The Americanization of the Homosexual.* New York: St. Martin's, 1982.

Borhek, Mary V. *Coming Out to Parents: A Two-way Survival Guide for Lesbians and Gay Men and Their Parents.* New York: Pilgrim Press, 1983.

Dannecker, Martin. *Theories of Homosexuality.* London: Gay Men's Press, 1981.

Fricke, Aaron. *Reflections of a Rock Lobster: A Story About Growing Up Gay.* Boston: Alyson Publications, 1981.

Gantz, Joe. *Whose Child Cries: Children of Gay Parents Talk About Their Lives.* Rolling Hills Estates, CA: Jalmar Press, 1983.

Gibson, E. Lawrence. *Get Off my Ship: Ensign Berg vs. the U.S. Navy.* New York: Avon, 1978.

Hall, Marny. *The Lavender Couch: A Consumer's Guide to Psychotherapy for Lesbians and Gay Men.* Boston: Alyson Publications, 1985.

Hanckel, Frances, and Cunningham, John. *A Way of Love, A Way of Life: A Young Person's Introduction to What It Means to Be Gay.* New York: Lothrop, 1979.

Simpson, Ruth. *From the Closet to the Courts: The Lesbian Transition.* New York: Penguin, 1977.

INDEX

Adolescents, homosexual vs. heterosexual, 4–5, 11–16, 39–43, 93–95. *See also* Teenagers
Adoption, by homosexuals, 28
Advocate, The (newspaper), 55
AIDS (Acquired Immune Deficiency Syndrome), 77–82; attitude toward victims of, 80–81; cause of, 78; early symptoms, 79; epidemic proportions of, 78, 79; information sources, 81–82; and opportunistic infections, 78; research funding, 91; susceptible groups, 78–79
AIDS Action Committee, 81
AIDS Action Line, 81
AIDS/KS Foundation, 81
AIDS Project/Los Angeles, 82
AIDS Risk Reduction Guidelines, 80
Alaska Gay Coalition, 87–88
Alexander the Great, 10
American Civil Liberties Union, 8
American Journal of Orthopsychiatry, 28
American Psychiatric Association, 8–9, 52–53, 54–55

American Psychological Association, 9
Anchorage, Alaska, Blue Book, 87–88
Animals, homosexuality in, 49
Ann Arbor, Michigan, 91
Antigay attitudes, 3, 17–21, 45–46, 50, 68. *See also* Discrimination
Aristotle, 10
Artificial insemination, 28
Aumiller, Richard, 86–87

Beach, Frank, 48–49
Bible, the, 18
Bowie, David, 10

California, gay rights in, 83–85, 91–92
California Supreme Court, 83–85
Cancer, AIDS and, 78
Careers of homosexuals, 9–10
Chicago, Illinois, 91
Child molestation, 9
Children of homosexuals, 28–34, 38; custody battles for, 34–38, 83
Christian doctrine on sex, 18, 45–46

INDEX

Gay Teachers, 9
Girls, upbringing of, 26–27
Grandparents, in custody battles, 36

Herpes simplex, 78
Heterosexuality, 2, 49; biological value of, 49, 50–51; as cultural norm, 45–46, 47–48, 49; as "medical norm," 47–48; as product of learning and conditioning, 47, 48, 51–52
Heterosexuals: and child molestation, 9; feeling threatened by gays, 19; and illegal sex acts, 8; mental adjustment compared to homosexuals, 50
High school, discrimination against homosexual students in, 30, 87
Homophobia, 17–21; defined, 17
Homosexuality: becoming aware of, 2–3, 11–14, 39–40; causes and factors of, 7, 47; "coming out," 3–4, 5, 15–16, 23–24; cultural/societal taboos, 3, 17–21, 45–46; defined, 2, 5–6; hiding, 3, 14–15, 16, 24–25, 40–43, 65–66, 71, 88; in history, 7, 18, 45; medical/psychiatric views of, 8–9, 46–55; statistics, 7; suppression of preference for, 7–8
Homosexual sex acts: church and, 18, 45–46; law and, 8, 54–55; percentage of men performing, 46
Hooker, Evelyn, 49–50
Housing discrimination, 54, 83
HTLV-3 virus, 78

Illinois, gay rights in, 91–92
Illness. See Pathological view of homosexuality

Immigration, 90
Infections, AIDS and, 78
Initiation rites, 48
Institute for Sex Research, 48
Insurance benefits, of marriage, 89–90

John, Elton, 10
Jokes about homosexuals, 3
Joplin, Janis, 10
Judiciary, the. See Court cases

Kaposi's sarcoma, 78
Kinsey, Alfred, 46–48

LAV (lymphademopathy-associated virus), 78
Law and homosexuality, 8, 18, 20, 54–55, 83–92. See also Civil rights; Court cases; Crime
Legislative redress, 54–55, 83, 88–89, 91–92; lobbying for, 91–92
Lesbians: children of, 28–34; custody battles against, 34–36; defined, 2; and men, misconceptions, 21; as mothers, 28–36; special problems of, 25–27; stories of, 11–16, 61–65, 93–95
Lewis, K., 29
Licensing, discrimination in, 54
Life styles, alternative, 8, 18–19, 23–33
Local legislation, 54–55, 91
Los Angeles, California, 91

Marnor, Judd, 51–52
Marriage, 1–2, 19–20, 27–28; denied to homosexuals, 83, 89–90; legal and economic advantages of, 20, 89–90; wife abuse in, 28

101

INDEX

Reproduction, 20–21, 50; church and, 18, 45–46
Rhode Island, 87
Romantic love, 1; among homosexuals, 2, 23; lesbian voice on, 1–16

San Francisco, California, 91
Sappho, 10
Sex education, 4
Sexual acts: homosexual, decriminalization of, 88; illegal, by heterosexuals vs. those of homosexuals, 8, 88; religious strictures on, 18, 45–46, 50, 51
Sexual orientation, 46–52; capacity for, 46–47; cultural/societal norms of, 45–46, 47–48; extremes of, 49; learned, 26, 47, 51–52; psychiatric attempt at changing, 47–48, 51
Shingles, 78
Singles life style, 33; homosexual, 23, 32–33; with children, 32–33
Skin cancer, 78
Smith, Bessie, 10
Social Work (journal), 29
Society. See Culture(s)
Spock, Benjamin, 26
State legislation, 54–55, 88–89, 91
Stereotypes of homosexuals, 2–3, 21, 40, 71, 73; affecting court decisions, 35–36, 37–38; media use of, 4; of women, 26
Stonewall Inn, New York, raid on, 91
Student organizations,

discrimination against, 83, 85–87
Survivor benefits, 89–90
Szaz, Thomas, 50–51, 52

Task Force on Homosexuality, 50
Tax benefits of marriage, 20, 89
Teachers: attitudes toward homosexuality, 30; homosexual, 83–85
Teenagers: and homosexuality of parent, 29–30; problems of homosexual minors, 93–95. See also Adolescents
Triangle Area Gay Scientists, 10
Tuberculosis, 78

University campuses, and gay rights, 85–87
University of Delaware, 86–87
University of Missouri, 85–86
U.S. Circuit Courts of Appeals, 86
U.S. District Courts, 86–87
U.S. Supreme Court, 38, 88

Virginia Commonwealth University, 86
Visitation rights, 36–37

Washington, D.C., 91
Washington Post, 55
Whitman, Walt, 10
Wife abuse, 26, 28
Williams, Tennessee, 10
Wisconsin, gay rights law, 91
Woolf, Virginia, 10
Workforce (lesbian group), 10

ABOUT THE AUTHOR

Elaine Landau received her B.A. degree from New York University in English and Journalism and a Master's degree in Library and Information Science from Pratt Institute.

She has worked as a newspaper reporter, an editor, and a librarian, but believes that many of her most fascinating as well as rewarding hours have been spent researching and writing books and articles on contemporary issues for young people.

Ms. Landau makes her home in New York City.